Tarikh

VOL. 6. NO. 1

Historical Method

GUEST EDITOR:
Robert Smith

EDITORS:
A. I. Asiwaju
Michael Crowder

Published for the
Historical Society of Nigeria

 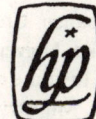

by Longman
and in the United States by Humanities Press

LONGMAN GROUP LIMITED
LONDON

*Associated companies, branches and
representatives throughout the world.
Distributed in the United States and
Canada by Humanities Press,
171 First Avenue,
Atlantic Highlands, New Jersey 07716, USA.*

© *Historical Society of Nigeria 1978*

*All rights reserved. No part of this
publication may be reproduced, stored
in a retrieval system, or transmitted in
any form or by any means, electronic,
mechanical, photocopying, recording,
or otherwise, without the prior permission of the Copyright owner.*

First published 1978

ISBN 0 582 60357 9

Printed in Hong Kong by
Wing King Tong Co Ltd

EDITORIAL OFFICE

Department of History, University of Lagos, Nigeria

ADVISORY EDITORIAL BOARD

Professor T. O. Ranger, University of Manchester
Dr(Mrs) A. B. Jones, Department of Education, Monrovia, Liberia
Professor B. A. Ogoto, University of Nairobi, Kenya
Dr(Mrs) F. Mahoney, Banjul, The Gambia
Professor J. D. Omer-Cooper, University of Otago
Professor A. A. Boahen, University of Ghana, Legon, Accra
Dr. M. S. Kiwanuka, University of Cambridge
Dr. R. Pankhurst, Institute of Ethiopian Studies, Addis Ababa
Mrs. Talabi Lucan, Ministry of Education, Freetown, Sierra Leone

Contents

	Page
Notes on Contributors	iv
Introduction by The Guest Editor	vii
Explanation in African history: how and why? by Robert Smith	1
The relationship between history and other disciplines by E. J. Alagoa	12
The uses of oral traditions in the writing of African history by Phillips Stevens, Jr.	21
Monocausal explanations in African history: A prevalent distortion by A. E. Afigbo	31
The Marxist approach to historical explanation by Robin Law	40
Historical explanation: the heresy of historicism by Jeremy White	51

Notes on Contributors

Professor A. E. Afigbo, Professor of History at the University of Nigeria, Nsukka, is the author of *The Warrant Chiefs: Indirect Rule in Southern Nigeria, 1891–1929*, as well as many articles on different aspects of West African history.

Professor E. J. Alagoa, until recently Professor of History and Director of the Centre for Cultural Studies at the University of Lagos, is the author of a general history of the Niger Delta and a history of Nembe-Brass as well as of articles mainly on Nigerian history. He has now moved to the new University of Port Harcourt, Nigeria, as first Head of the History Department there.

Robin Law, a Lecturer in History at the University of Stirling in Scotland, is the author of articles on West Africa, especially Yoruba history. His book on the Oyo Empire was published by the Oxford University Press in 1977.

Phillips Stevens, Jr, is Associate Professor in the Department of Anthropology at the State University of New York at Buffalo. He has published articles on aspects of pre-colonial West African history and culture, and a book on the stone sculptures of Esie, in the Kwara State of Nigeria.

Jeremy White is a Senior Lecturer in the Department of History at the University of Lagos who specialises in Political Philosophy and the Philosophy of History. He has published articles and presented papers on various aspects of the latter.

Robert Smith was the first acting head of the Department of History in the University of Ife, Nigeria and is now a Senior Lecturer in the University of Ibadan. His publications include *Yoruba Warfare in the Nineteenth Century* (with Professor J. F. A. Ajayi), *Kingdoms of the Yoruba,* and *Warfare and Diplomacy in Pre-Colonial West Africa*; his book on *The Lagos Consulate* is to be published in 1978.

Acknowledgements

The publishers are grateful to the following for permission to reproduce photographs:

Africana Museum for pages 5 (left) and 54; Professor E. J. Alagoa for pages 14, 15, 16, 18 and 22; Camera Press Ltd. for pages 41 (top left, top right and bottom), 57 (left), 58 (top right and bottom) and 60; Mary Evans Picture Library for page 52; Alan Hutchinson Library for page 37; Mansell Collection for page 5 (right); Popperfoto for pages 6, 8, 57 (right) and 58 (top left); Radio Times Hulton Picture Library for pages 26, 44 and 48.

The cover represents dominant figures of history—Shaka (top left), Nkrumah, Mosheshwe (bottom left) and Menelik, with Marx in the centre. The photographs were kindly supplied by Africana Museum, Mansell Collection and Popperfoto.

The maps were drawn by Neil Hyslop.

Introduction

In his pursuit of any form of knowledge, it is helpful for the student to stand back from time to time from his subject and to reflect upon the general nature of his activities. Can he justify, to himself and to others, his expenditure of time and effort? How does his subject relate to other subjects, and his discipline to other disciplines? Can he improve upon his work in both his means of setting about it—his research—and the presentation of his findings? Such introspection, though it has its dangers like other forms of self-questioning, is a healthy supplement to scholarship, for, without the perspective which it gives, learning can degenerate into provincialism, and history, to particularise, into antiquarianism.

The intention of this present number of *Tarikh* relates primarily to the last of the questions above, thus emphasising the practical rather than the philosophical aspects of the writing of history (that is, of 'historiography', to use a word which differentiates the recovery of the past from the past itself), in the hope that both students and their teachers may benefit. Nevertheless, the enterprise, as the reader will quickly perceive, can hardly avoid some involvement with philosophical issues. It is, however, no bad thing to be reminded that history is not only an arrangement of facts ('one damn thing—or king—after another', as it has been called) and that the interpretation of historical events and situations must be preceded and accompanied by a measure of abstract reasoning. This makes it especially important to warn readers of this number of the differences in outlook which were and are bound to arise in a collection of articles by six authors whose views about the rationale of their discipline are likely to vary as much as, and often more than, their views on the more practical questions of 'how' and 'why'. Indeed, the last two articles were deliberately invited in order to offer a contrast in points of view.

In planning the number, the editor has attempted to cover within the limits set by the substantive editors of *Tarikh* what seemed to him the essential elements in historical method. But the subject is a wide one and it was by no means unexpected that the resulting articles, despite the breadth of their scope, omit much which might be held to be relevant. For example, the process of writing history has many pitfalls apart from that important fallacy of monocausality described by Professor Afigbo. Fallacies of language, and especially the dogmatic attitude which leads to the writing of 'all' where (in the absence of precise statistics) only 'a majority' or perhaps just 'some' would be justified, could well have made the subject of another article, and there are many other forms of determinism than the 'heresy' examined here by Dr White. As to 'precise statistics', the historian should use these wherever possible since he must always be asking 'how many?', but he must also bear in mind that they tell only a part of a story—and he should not commit the ugly stylistic absurdity of writing '50 per cent.' instead of 'half'! Again, a still more down-to-earth type of article might have been included to explain the different forms taken by historical works with

Introduction

their different methods of setting out references and the rest of the critical apparatus which authenticates debatable points (or, in displaying the evidence, allows the thoughtful reader to reach other conclusions on the same premises). This would have been perhaps the most difficult and tedious article to write and to read since the theme is both dry and has many variations; the best advice which it could give can be put very shortly: to study and then to follow as models those works of scholarship which seem to the novice historian himself to relay their 'message' with the greatest clarity, precision, conviction and (since history is art as well as science) elegance.

The editor, aware of these shortcomings, hopes that this number will nevertheless stimulate its readers by its faults and omissions as well as by its virtues to reflect upon the general nature of the discipline which it is their privilege to practise, and will help them in preparing, planning and presenting their work.

R.S.S.

Tarikh Orders and Subscriptions

New and back numbers of *Tarikh* are obtainable through your local bookseller or from your local Longman office; in North America from Humanities Press.

Alternatively subscriptions can be taken out by prepayment for four issues plus postage.

In USA and Canada: to Humanities Press Inc., 171 First Avenue, Atlantic Highlands, N.J. 07716

In Africa, Britain and elsewhere: to Longman Group Ltd., Longman House, Burnt Mill, Harlow, Essex, UK

Subscription

Please enter my subscription for four issues to *Tarikh* beginning with ....

....

I enclose payment for four issues and postage/please bill me.

Name ....

Address ....

....

Tarikh Order Form

Already published

Leadership in 19th Century Africa	1.1	☐
African Leadership and European Domination	1.2	☐
Man in Africa	1.3	☐
Modernisers in Africa	1.4	☐
Early Christianity in Africa	2.1	☐
African Achievement and Tragedy	2.2	☐
Six Aspects of African History	2.3	☐
France in Africa	2.4	☐
Christianity in Modern Africa	3.1	☐
The Peoples of Uganda in the 19th Century	3.2	☐
Indirect Rule in British Africa	3.3	☐
Independence Movements in Africa 1	3.4	☐
Independence Movements in Africa 2	4.1	☐
Government in Pre-Colonial Africa	4.2	☐
European Conquest and African Resistance 1	4.3	☐
European Conquest and African Resistance 2	4.4	☐
Peoples and Kingdoms of West Africa in the Pre-Colonial Period	5.1	☐
Egypt and the Nile Valley	5.2	☐
Protest Against Colonial Rule in West Africa	5.3	☐
The African Diaspora	5.4	☐

To (Bookseller/Publisher)

Please supply the issues of *Tarikh* ticked above.

Name ....

Address ....

....

Explanation in African History: How and Why?

Robert Smith

'I wish he would explain his Explanation'—Byron

As with most branches of learning, history is concerned with the explanation of how and why certain events and situations (to be referred to subsequently as the *explanandum*) have come about, of both change and stability. In the case of history, this concern is directed to the past, and to the past of human beings. In the title of this article, the neutral word 'explanation' is used rather than 'causation' since this does not imply the determinist view that the *explanandum* was the inevitable result of the elements which make up the explanation (the *explanans*)—that it could only have happened in this way and that this was the only possible result. Another point about the title is that the qualification of the noun 'history' by the adjective 'African' means no more than that the problem of historical explanation is to be discussed in an African setting; it does not mean that African history differs in any essential way from the history of any other part of the world—history is history!

As African history shares the general character of all history, so it also shares its purpose. This, despite the many elaborate justifications which have been advanced for the study of history, can be summed up as being that of all other branches of knowledge, the pursuit of truth, in this case specifically the pursuit of truth about the past of human beings and their institutions, which requires both a setting aside so far as possible of all prejudice and the exercise of empathy, the sensitive and imaginative effort to understand past societies and events in their own terms. The historian's quest not only requires the establishment of what were the events of the past—what happened—but also their explanation (how and why these events came to pass) and their assessment (how important were they). Beyond these duties there lies the possibility of extracting from the past lessons for the present and future, and therefore means of helping humanity in the understanding and handling of its problems. These lessons are given primarily by means of specific instances but are sometimes also formulated in generalisations. The status of such generalisations is discussed in those articles in this issue which are concerned with aspects of determinism, but it may be said here that they are not laws but statements of possibilities or at best probabilities, and also that the 'lessons' of history often seem to point in different directions.

The historian's main approach to his problem of explaining the past takes the form of answers to questions which ask, explicitly or implicitly, 'how?' and 'why?'. (The historian's third form of question about the *explanandum*, which begins with 'How important?', is left aside here since assessment of the *explanandum*, as distinct from that of the *explanans*, is not strictly a part of explanation.) In answering 'how?', a narration is called for in which the events or separate series of events leading to the *explanandum* are described in a coherent, usually chronological sequence. The older (in the sense of 'senior') style of history is sometimes described as 'narrative history'. The description applies, for example, to Johnson's *History of the Yorubas* or Egharevba's *Short History of Benin*, and to virtually the whole range of 'classical' historians: to Herodotus or Livy in ancient times or Clarendon or Gibbon in seventeenth and eighteenth-century England. The demand for such narrative history has been recently alleged (by J. H. Plumb) to be dead or dying, but this is belied by the evidence of publishers' lists and libraries. In no sense can narrative history be dismissed as out of date, for before we can ask why any change took place or any situation came about, we must know, so far as we can, what were the relevant events and in what order these took place—that is, we must establish the absolute and also relative chronology, the dates of these events, so that they can be placed alongside and compared with events elsewhere. The importance to be attributed to narrative and to chronology in particular is illustrated by the efforts to recover the pre-colonial history of West Africa—for example, to determine the order and the dates (usually given according to the Western Calendar) of the events leading to the fall of Old Oyo, the Yoruba capital in Western Nigeria, in or about 1837. Only when the narrative is know in some detail can the historian hope to tackle seriously the questions which begin 'why'.

The answers to 'why' are usually referred to as the 'analysis', or as analytical as opposed to narrative history. In an analysis the facts or events of the underlying narrative are transposed into the reasons or causes (but for philosophers the latter word has a determinist connotation) or factors (a word disliked by some historians) which form the elements of the explanation, and chronology is subordinated to the marshalling of these in an order which clarifies their relative importance—relative, that is, to each other and to the *explanandum*. This order varies; some historians prefer an ascending order which leads up to and puts last the most important factors, others prefer to begin with the most important and to add the rest in a descending order—somewhat as in a procession in church the Bishop walks last, whereas at a military parade the commanding officer heads his troops. Most articles in journals of academic history are written in this analytical way and so are those important (but sometimes rather forbidding) books termed 'monographs'. An example of such a book is Lawrence Stone's *The Causes of the English Revolution* (1972) in which the stirring events of the wars in seventeenth-century England are entirely omitted, the author assuming that his readers already know this background and concentrating instead on a dissection, comparison and assessment of the factors which (he claims) explain these wars.

But in practice the difference between the two approaches, the narrative and the analytical, is far from absolute. Most history combines the two, and can be classified by the approach to which it more closely adheres. Indeed, it is one of the characteristics of a succesful historian that he welds together narrative with analysis into a unity. Such combinations can be illustrated from most of the books in the Ibadan or Legon History Series, an illustration which probably reflects the special position of the history of tropical Africa in that, coupled with an ever-increasing interest in answering the 'why' questions about the African past, there is the need to recover a factual narrative which has frequently not yet been recorded in ways acceptable to professional historians. Consider, for example, the well known question 'Was Uthman dan Fodio's jihad a religious, political or economic movement?', which can only be answered by establishing the sequence of events, combining narrative with analysis.

Not only does analytical history require a basis, explicit or implicit, of narrative, but even the most purely narrative form of history can be shown to contain a good deal of implied analysis. There are two important reasons for this. The first is that the historian is usually confronted with a mass of evidence of possible relevance to his topic (this may be rather less true of the pre-colonial history of tropical Africa than of many other parts of the world), much of which he jettisons before selecting what he judges to have a direct bearing on his theme or some part of it. Discarding and selecting like this is the first step in analysis, for in choosing to describe or simply to refer to certain events or situations and to eliminate others, the historian is already suggesting answers to 'why' as well as to 'how' questions. Secondly, any kind of history requires the use of words (even a silent enactment would do so at the preparatory stage), and not only must these words be selected, but they also constitute in themselves a classification of, and thus a judgment upon, whatever is being described. Consider, for example, what is evoked by and implicit in the use of the different but related terms 'revolution', 'revolt', and 'coup', which not only describe and classify such events, and thereby analyse them, but also suggest comparisons with an immense range of other events which occurred at other times and in other places and which have been similarly described.

Nevertheless, the broad distinction between a narrative and an analytical explanation remains useful, and it is with this second approach that the rest of this article is mainly concerned, since it is by analysis that the historian can most economically and most convincingly demonstrate what the evidence has led him to believe is the truth about the particular section of the past with which he is dealing. The next point to notice, then, is that in answering 'why?' the historian is rarely, almost never, content to adduce only one explanatory factor. Even though he may conclude that one factor far outweighs all others in bringing about the *explanandum*, he will look for other factors which interacted with, delayed, stimulated, or perhaps 'triggered off' his grand single factor. But it is much more usual to find that a multiplicity of factors must be adduced, each in itself the result of a separate chain of development. To master all this material, classification is required, and such familiar labels as 'political', 'economic', 'ideological' and the like play their (overlapping) parts. But containing and transcending all such divisions, the historian needs, consciously or unconsciously, openly or by stylistic concealment, to categorise his material according to the different levels at which it occurs. Such categorisations differ from one historian to another, both in the descriptions which they use and in the degree of differentiation between levels, but the principle remains the same. One simple approach towards explaining, for example, the problem presented by event y (the *explanandum*) is to distinguish between

1. Long-term (or situational or dispositional) factors, which brought about a situation in which y became *possible*.
2. Medium-term or median factors which brought about a situation in which y became *probable*.
3. Occasions, or 'triggers', the factors (which in this case are nearly always the action or actions of one person or more) which made y all but *certain*—'all but certain' rather than 'certain' because bullets may go wide, fuses may die out before reaching the powder barrel, and so on.

The construction of such a 'morphology' (to use Elton's term) of explanation does not complete this preliminary to the historian's task. His responsibility, as already indicated, is to establish an order of importance among the factors which he adduces. And here it must be noted that what he identifies as his most important factors may occur at any of the levels of explanation which he postulates, though they are most likely to be found at the first two in the suggested morphology above.

What has now been described must by no means be taken as an account of the historian's final product which concludes his explanation. A morphology is useful in sorting, assessing and ordering the evidence for an historical event, and then for the making of the plan or outline which precedes the written account and examination; it is something like the scaffolding which is erected on a building site, and it needs to be clothed with words, its concepts must be fitted into each other so as to create a unity; in summary, it must be given persuasive literary form, for as Miss C. V. Wedgwood has written, 'History ... is an art, like all the other sciences'. The life of man is continuous and unified, all its aspects overlapping, and it is this reality which the artist-historian tries to convey by reassembling the material on which the scientist-historian has imposed an artificial separation. Thus the final form of the historian's explanation will depend partly on his assessment of the relative importance of the factors adduced and partly on aesthetic considerations. It will also reflect his philosophic approach, whether 'nomothetic', aiming at the establishment of general 'laws', or 'idiographic', seeking to understand unique events and situations, though even in the latter case he is unlikely to resist making a few summarising generalisations.

Turning now to the materials of the historian's explanation, the 'bricks' which must clothe the scaffolding (to continue the metaphor of the last paragraph), the first point to notice is its multifarious, almost unconfined nature, comprising an area of enormous potential relevance, for a case can always be made out for the inter-relatedness of factors which at first sight appear remote in time, space and character from each other. Reverting to the 'familiar labels' referred to earlier, such topics can never be treated in isolation. For a 'political' event, many non-

Explanation in African History: How and Why?

Mosheshwe (*left*) and Menelik: great men of history

political factors—economic, military, ideological, and so on—must be taken into account alongside strictly political factors. Within the limits of this article it is not possible to examine in detail this vast field, but a few matters require comment.

First, since history concerns the past of human beings, the question arises as to the extent to which the historian should look for his explanations in the lives, personalities and motives of individuals—the theory that, as Carlyle put it, 'history is the biography of great men'; men like Mosheshwe, Dan Fodio, Shaka, or Menelik. This 'greatness', it must be noted, does not in this context denote moral greatness or carry any sense of approval, but refers rather to the extent to which the individual concerned (a hero to some perhaps, a villain to others) influenced or even dominated the history of his own and perhaps also of subsequent times. Thus, Clarendon could write of Cromwell as '... a great bad man', and doubtless the same sort of judgment would be passed by some Yoruba historians on Bashorun Gaha who overshadowed the Alafins of eighteenth-century Oyo, or on Afonja whose ambitions opened a way for the Fulani into Yorubaland.

This concept of the role of the 'Great Man' in history has been strongly contested, for example by Marx who saw such men as no more than representatives of powerful forces which they did not control. Few historians except the Marxists would go so far as to agree that Great Men can be reduced to puppets in this way, but it is now widely accepted that biography constitutes only an adjunct to history, valuable but restricted in range. Nevertheless, the historian still has to come to terms with these dominant figures, and in narrative history

Explanation in African History: How and Why?

Kwame Nkrumah: crowd dominator

especially they still loom large. One lesson which might be derived from such views, determinist in character, like those mentioned above, and of which the Marxists are representative, is that Great Men can be classified as being of two main types: those who are great by their ability to seize the opportunities of their age, to go with and then to dominate the crowd by summing up and feeding their aspirations (Nkrumah is perhaps an example here), and those lonely and usually

Explanation in African History: How and Why?

tragic figures (like Solzhenitsyn) whose work is carried out or whose message is given in spite of and against the forces of their day. But when it comes to applying this scheme to individuals, the categorisation soon tends to break down. Consider any of the Great Men of African history and it will be seen that often they not only summed up forces which can be distinguished in their times but were also the focus of opposition by quite other forces. History is a complex undertaking, and the historian must beware of attractive approaches which simplify what is not, and should not be portrayed as being, simple.

Though the role of Great Men has perhaps been exaggerated in much historical writing even in recent times, it still remains true that it is with human beings, whether great or humble, that history is concerned. These men, our ancestors, can and indeed must be considered under very different aspects: as individual leaders, as individual representatives, and as groups (like governments or states), and in every case the historian will find himself confronted by what is probably the most difficult of all his tasks in explanation: the determination of motive. To account for human actions, even in the present day, is hazardous, and for the historian to make statements about the intentions of the actors in his account, whether individuals or groups, and the reasoning and inner promptings behind those actions, plunges him into the deepest of deep water. This has been greatly complicated by the demonstrations of Freud and later psychologists that man's conduct is influenced (again both as an individual and as a group) by motives which are unconscious, and so unrecognised by him at the time of action (and probably ever afterwards), as well as by conscious motives, the former being often, perhaps always, the more important. With the progress of psychology towards the status of a science, more information continues to emerge about motive, but the results tend often to obscure rather than to clarify the situation, as recent essays in 'psycho-history' show. Yet historians seem unable to escape from the discussion, in such depth as they can, of motive, while intellectual history, or the history of ideas, has been able, with some help from the psychologists, to make important contributions to our understanding of past events and actions. For example, topics such as the abolition of the slave trade, the partition of Africa, and the spread of colonialism are all dealt with very largely in terms of what was *intended* by the European powers, personified as Britain, France, Germany and the rest. It is also important for the historian to distinguish between the pretexts which are alleged for human actions and policies and the 'real', often quite different, motives which may lie behind them, a task adding another dimension to the morphology outlined above. Finally, the irony which makes up so much of history emerges clearly in the failure of men's actions to produce those results which they intended.

Another problem which besets the historian's attempts to explain the past is how to take account of incidents which from their nature are described (by contemporaries and subsequently) as 'accidental' or 'contingent'. But the definition of an accident is elusive, for it is impossible to envisage events or situations which cannot be explained in some way. E. H. Carr in *What is History?* describes the concept as one of 'two savoury red herrings'—laid

Sigmund Freud: unconscious motives

presumably across the trail of the hunter-historian to put him off the scent as he draws the historical coverts. Efforts to pin down the concept (to vary the metaphor) have been made by philosophers of history: Ernest Nagel, notably, has isolated four main uses of the term 'accident'. To the present writer, these definitions can conveniently be reduced to two categories. First, there is the view that history (and it may be added life generally) is an irrational, meaningless series of events which are only superficially connected, a mere 'chapter of accidents' which it is hardly worth attempting to explain. This view (one which is peculiarly infuriating to determinists) is by no means so rare as might be thought, even among professional historians; A. J. P. Taylor comes near to it in some of his pronouncements on the origins of the Second World War, as did H. A. L. Fisher in his famous (or notorious) Preface to his *History of Europe*:

> I can see only one emergency following upon another as wave follows upon wave, only one great fact with respect to which, since it is unique, there can be no generalizations, only one safe rule for the historian: that he should recognize in the development of human destinies the play of the contingent and the unforeseen.

As with other forms of philosophical scepticism, it is difficult to find a wholly convincing answer to such views, so that the empirical demonstration that our explanations work and can in a sense be repeated must serve as the basis of historical reconstruction just as it is the basis on which the rest of human life is organised. Thus it is with the second main category of accident that the historian is likely to be most seriously concerned. This comprises those events and situations which, first, were unforeseen (except perhaps as remote possibilities, as matters going awry or out of control) by contemporaries, and which secondly were unforeseeable (again, except as remote possibilities) in the contemporary state of knowledge (for example, the spread of the Black Death in fourteenth-century Europe, when medical knowledge was more restricted than it is today); thirdly, they were also unmotivated, at any rate in the context of the *explanandum*. This second category does constitute a real issue for the historian and one which, whenever it occurs, he needs to take into account in his explanatory thesis.

A third aspect of historical explanation which needs some comment is that of conditional causation. Historians occasionally write of certain events or situations as having been either 'sufficient' or 'necessary' causes or causal factors in bringing about an *explanandum*. By this they imply, in the first case, that *if* a certain factor was present, then the *explanandum* was a necessary consequence, though one which could have come about in other ways. In the second case, they imply that *only if* that factor was present could the *explanandum* have come about, though it might still not have happened. A third possibility is the biconditional one, introduced, at least by implication, with the words '*if and only if*.' Statements of this kind commit the writer by their nature to a determinist view of history and there may seem little point in amending the concept by adding words like 'probably' or 'possibly': 'if x then probably y' etc., where it is the known past which is the subject. But this approach does at times help to direct the historian towards his evidence. It can be particularly useful where evidence about the past is largely lacking and the historian is speculating (it can hardly be called more than that) on the basis of contemporary facts such as climatic indications or surviving artifacts. But conditional statements have their main use as statements about the future, that is, in prediction, and the terms 'necessary' and 'sufficient' are usually better avoided by historians in describing the factors which they adduce in their explanations of the past.

It will have been noticed that throughout this article references have been made to determinist and, by implication, anti-determinist views of history. Determinism is linked by E. H. Carr with accident as one of the two 'red herrings' in the historian's way, side-issues which should not be allowed to distract him from his main task. But determinism is surely much more than this since the form taken by any historical explanation hinges on whether the process being described is conceived as leading 'inevitably', 'unavoidably', 'inexorably', or any similar word, to the *explanandum*. Since determinism is a topic in other articles in this issue (notably that by Jeremy White), the subject will not be laboured further here, except to add that to have attempted to sum up the problems of historical explanation without at least some mention of such views would have been like a performance of *Hamlet* without the Prince.

Perhaps the most important point to emerge from this present study of explanation is one that is obvious enough but not trivial: that history is a great deal more complicated a matter than many laymen think! To his 'why' questions (less so to his 'how?'), the non-professional usually expects a simple answer, roughly in the form that 'x caused y' ($x \rightarrow y$). Conversely, the characteristic of the historian, as we have seen, is to expect to find more than one factor to explain y, after which he will examine the points of interaction between his factors and will assess their degree of importance relative to y, his *explanandum*. Nor will he be satisfied until he has explored the field of probabilities and possibilities as widely as possible and thoroughly tested all his hypotheses. This is not to claim that the historian wants to shut out the amateur or the interested layman or to over-professionalise his craft, but rather that history in its dual aspect of art and science, seeking the truth about the human past, dedicated to both objectivity and empathy, demands a discipline no less rigorous than is demanded by, say, physics or linguistics. Finally, since truth is never totally attainable, history remains, as had been said, an 'unending debate', and the historian's role can never be exhausted. This does not imply that historical controversies can never be resolved, but rather that as new evidence and new ways of looking at the past continue to emerge, new controversies will continue to arise. Such controversy is of great value and importance to the recovery of the past, but only so long as it is conducted in an open-minded yet critical spirit which constantly admits the possibility that the controversialist's most deeply-rooted convictions as well as his most carefully conceived hypotheses may have to be discarded in the light of the evidence. Ranke, the German apostle of objective history, sought to discover 'how things really happened', a noble aspiration which Oakeshott, the English idealist philosopher, takes a stage further when he writes of the historian's goal as being what 'the evidence obliges us to believe'.

For further reading

A convenient introduction is:
>GARDINER P., ed., *The Philosophy of History*, Oxford, 1974.

Two more general books:
>CARR, E. H. *What is History?* London, 1961.
>ELTON, G. R. *The Practice of History*, London, 1969.

Using the decline and fall of Old Oyo, the Yoruba capital in Western Nigeria, as an illustration, the following articles may be useful:
>AKINJOGBIN, I. A. 'The Oyo Empire in the Eighteenth Century', *Journal of the Historical Society of Nigeria,* iii, 3, 1966.
>ATANDA, J. A. 'The Fall of the Old Oyo Empire: a reconsideration of its cause', *Journal of the Historical Society of Nigeria,* v, 4, 1971.
>LAW, R. C. C. 'The constitutional troubles of Oyo in the eighteenth century', *Journal of African History*, xii, 1, 1971.
>SMITH, ROBERT 'Event and Portent: The fall of Old Oyo, a problem in historical explanation', *Africa,* xli, 3, 1971.

The Relationship Between History and Other Disciplines

E. J. Alagoa

Introduction

History may be defined as the study of man through the evidence of his past actions. It is a discipline that must of necessity embrace aspects of several other disciplines which are able to contribute to an understanding of man by means of what he has attempted or accomplished in the past. Since man has adapted his life to the physical environment or tried to adapt the environment to his needs by the development of technology, even disciplines in the physical and biological sciences have a bearing on history. And it may be taken for granted that every discipline concerned with specialised aspects of human life and activity must be relevant to the history of man in his totality. Thus all the disciplines in the Humanities dealing with the mental, spiritual, and physical aspects of human development must be relevant to a degree in a comprehensive view of historical studies.

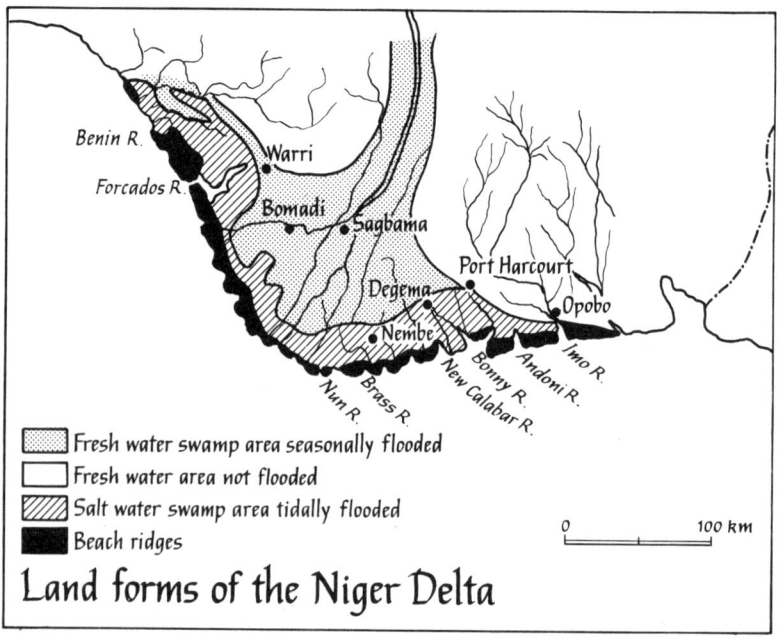

Land forms of the Niger Delta

The comprehensive view of history should not be taken to imply that all other disciplines are subsidiary to history. Rather, it indicates the essential unity of all knowledge, especially when such knowledge relates to a study of man. Further, it means that just as other disciplines are required for a full and satisfactory historical understanding, history constitutes an important ingredient of other humanistic studies. This unitary view of knowledge was of course, the tradition among such early civilisations as the Greek; and most African societies did not, traditionally, distinguish and partition knowledge into compartments. In this scientific age, it has become the fashion to create specialisations out of the study of different perspectives of the human condition or the physical environment. The point of this article, however, is that the various disciplines are still interdependent and, in particular, that the historian cannot alone answer all the questions that he must ask in the pursuit of his vocation.

In the historical study of man, differences in orientation, perspective, as well as specialisation are recognised. These internal differences also indicate relationships with particular disciplines. Thus, in the study of African history, the emphasis was at first on political history, that is, the growth and history of states, and the nature and effects of colonialism. Recently, there has arisen a greater interest in economic history, the study of social institutions, and cultural phenomena, even in stateless societies. These perspectives to history suggest relationships to such disciplines as political science, economics, sociology, and anthropology.

So practitioners of these types of history require knowledge of the techniques and methodologies of these other disciplines in order to exploit the relevant and often specialised documents.

Other relations between history and other disciplines derive from theories of history, or views of the ways in which human action can best be studied and understood. Thus, some historians believe that changes of direction in historical movements are determined by the actions of great men. To such historians, the study of biography must be important in order to discover the ways in which the thoughts and actions of such great men shaped the destinies of nations. In such studies of individual men, a knowledge of the principles of psychology and even of psychiatry becomes relevant. Similarly, historians who believe in other types of forces that determine the direction of historical development require knowledge of other disciplines concerned with man in society, economic forces, or the influence of the environment and ecology.

Finally, historians seek the assistance of other disciplines in order to obtain full benefit from unusual documents. Thus, the difficulties of penetrating the distant past of African societies through oral traditions, literature, ethnographic data, and ancient artifacts have imposed on African historians the necessity of an inter-disciplinary or multi-disciplinary approach. It is now generally agreed that the earlier history of most African societies can best be reconstructed through the combined use of insights from Archaeology, Linguistics, Anthropology, and other disciplines. The reason is, of course, the absence of the written documents on which historians of societies with a long

The Relationship Between History and Other Disciplines

A fishing village between the Brass and St Nicholas river estuaries

Typical vegetation in this area

The Relationship Between History and Other Disciplines

Fishing village with dense mangrove forest behind

Close-up of the swamp forest, showing the characteristic roots of the red mangrove (*Rhizophora racemosa*)

tradition of literacy rely for an understanding of the past. Since African history is so well suited to the multi-discipline approach, the following examples will be taken in large part from African history.

History and the environmental sciences
We may take Geography as representative of the disciplines which assist the historian to understand the spatial and physical factors in human life. Historians who take a long time-perspective, that is, prehistorians, have been most aware of geographical factors in human history. Thus in European prehistory the importance of climatic changes has been realised, and the successive ice ages over Europe have been studied in detail. A comparative climatic change affecting historical development in Africa would be the effect of the drying up of the Sahara which resulted in the migration of many peoples from that vast area of Africa some six thousand years ago. However, a closer parallel to the European ice ages in African prehistory are the East African pluvials (what may be termed water ages), that is, periods when the lake levels rose, and wet, lush conditions prevailed. Within Nigeria alone, we can observe the possible effects of geogra-

Riverside farm, with forest in the background, a fishing camp in foreground

A village in a fresh-water delta

phical factors in the history of peoples living in such parts as the savannah regions of the far north, the mountains of the Jos plateau, or the watery swamplands of the Niger Delta. On a wider view, we can still see today the different ways of life imposed by geography on inhabitants of the polar regions of the world, in the temperate lands, and in the hot humid tropics.

We may take one example of historical reconstruction and interpretation using environmental factors. Even in the restricted area of the Niger Delta, there are three distinct ecological zones: the coastal sandy beach ridges, the salt-water swamp, and the fresh-water swamp. A survey of the oral traditions of the Niger Delta indicated that a majority of the inhabitants of the salt-water delta had migrated from the fresh-water swamp. Accordingly, the differences in the historical development of communities in the two zones was seen to derive in great part from the necessity to adapt to the different ecological systems. For example, the salt-water delta could only support fishing, salt-boiling, and trading communities. The communities in the fresh-water delta could farm as well as fish, and did not have to rely on trading with other communities.

History and Archaeology

When historians try to go very far back into the past, they often find their traditional sources no longer adequate to answer all the questions they wish to ask. Thus, even in parts of the world where written documentary evidence is the prime source, we discover that this source covers a comparatively brief period of the history of man on earth. This problem is even more acute in Africa where we have to rely on orally transmitted evidence. The difficulty with oral traditions has been that they can rarely supply reliable evidence over an extensive time span and in such circumstances the historian turns to the archaeologist for evidence of human activity from the distant past through digging into the earth for things made by man, or even parts of human beings which have been preserved.

In Africa especially, the concrete, visual evidence of archaeological artifacts has been very important as a supplement and corrective to the meagre evidence of oral traditions. It is not possible to argue against the artifact, and the earlier statements of European visitors that Africa did not produce advanced civilisations have been disproved by the discovery of fine works of art at such places as Nok, Ife, Benin, and Igbo Ukwu in Nigeria; large architectural structures in Zimbabwe; and of course, the abundant remains of the civilisation of the Nile Valley.

In terms of time dimension, archaeologists in East Africa have recovered the fossils of skeletons which suggest that man might have developed in this part of Africa over a million years ago. These discoveries give support to speculations that Africa was the cradle of man. In any case, Africa is now known to be one of the places in the world where man first took shape and developed the first stone tools, the basis of technology.

We may note that the evidence of oral tradition, written documents, and archaeological artifacts often overlap and are used together in reconstructions of

The author (Professor Alagoa) and Dr. Fred Anozie of the Archaeology Department at the University of Nigeria, Nsukka, cleaning the area round a skeleton in an excavation at Onyama in the Niger Delta

The author and Dr. Anozie discussing a decorated pot excavated from the same site

the past. Thus, in many parts of Africa, oral traditions indicate sites of old settlements to be excavated. And after objects have been brought out of such excavations, the oral traditions of local people are an important source of information on their possible uses and significance.

History and Linguistics
The study of languages and their relationships is a very fruitful means of learning about culture change and contact in the past. The study of loan words, for example, can show in what ways the speakers of one language have been related to another culture from which their language has borrowed items. Thus, through the analysis of Kanuri loan-words in Hausa, Joseph Greenberg was able to indicate the ways in which the Borno kingdom had exercised influence on the Hausa states in the past. It appears that the Hausa had obtained several of their political titles from Kanuri. Similarly, they learnt about writing and other aspects of culture derived ultimately from the Arab world through Kanuri, showing a major route by which Islamic influences penetrated Hausaland. Another example of the study of names and loan-words is the case of food plants in the Niger Delta, examined by Kay Williamson of the University of Port Harcourt. She has shown that common crops like cassava arrived in the Niger Delta from South America through the Portuguese. They appear to have arrived first in the western delta, and penetrated to the central and eastern delta through the influence of Benin-related groups, such as the Itsekiri, and others.

Another way in which linguistics has already proved its relevance to African history is in the area of language classification. Joseph Greenberg and Guthrie have demonstrated some of the historical inferences that can be drawn from similarities and differences between languages and dialects in their studies of Bantu. But the differences in the conclusions of these two linguists also show that no discipline has achieved the perfection of methodology that would lead to unanimity among its practitioners. According to Greenberg, the ancestors of the Bantu of Central, Eastern and Southern Africa came from the region of the Niger-Cameroon border. Guthrie believes that the Bantu heartland lies in the Katanga area of the Republic of Zaire.

Linguists have also attempted to reconstruct the vocabularies of long-extinct mother forms of existing languages. Thus Guthrie used his reconstructions of proto-Bantu to suggest the stage of cultural development reached by its speakers. It would appear that the ancestral Bantu were agriculturalists and could work iron.

A further development of the study of the processes of language change over time has led to the use of linguistics for dating. This aspect of linguistics, that is lexico-statistics and glotto-chronology, promises a great deal for African history. Thus, through the analysis of two related languages on the basis of a standard list of words, it is possible to estimate how long ago they were separated from a common stock. Thus, the Igala, Idoma and Yoruba became separate languages about two thousand years ago; and Ijo of the Niger Delta is some five thousand years distant from Igbo, Edo, and Yoruba.

History and the Social and Physical Sciences

The contribution of the Social Sciences is fairly easy to understand, since they supply theories and generalisations about the operation of society and processes of change, which are the subject of history. Such generalisations supply insights that prove useful to historians looking for bases for explanations for complex events. Anthropologists have built up a number of historical models in Africa, some of which have stimulated productive reconstructions by historians, but not all of them have been generally accepted.

It is a little more difficult to realise that other scientific disciplines can have a bearing on history. However, it is fairly easy to see the relevance to history of the study of the domestication of animals and crops. The biological sciences are relevant in such studies of the history of agriculture. Thus, when we hear that the Ethiopian Highlands and the bend of the Niger could have been early centres of crop domestication, it is possible to think of them also as early centres of population and civilisation. And, of course, irrigation agriculture was one cornerstone of the civilisation of the Nile Valley. And the yam and oil palm were a part of the history of the forest lands of the West African coast.

The medical sciences have also been used in African history to study the relationships between peoples, through blood-groups and typology. The study of disease patterns and epidemics also have a bearing on the growth of population, and the fertility and virility of populations. Some diseases of the past can be diagnosed from skeletons or mummies (in Egypt).

In more recent times the mathematical sciences too have gradually come to play a part in historical studies, especially Economic History. Studies of the slave trade, for example, have included statistical elements in an attempt to estimate the total numbers of Africans taken over to the Americas, or the effect of such population movements on the growth of population and historical development in Africa. American historians, in particular, have also experimented with the use of computers as well in the service of history.

Conclusion

It is possible to list many more disciplines that are related to history. The examples given are merely a selection aimed at showing that history is not an isolated discipline. For while historians practise their vocation with a great deal of autonomy and use other disciplines without permitting them to take over the interpretation of historical events and processes, the search for knowledge and the truth of the past of man is a cooperative enterprise in which many disciplines work together as interdependent units.

For further reading

ALAGOA, E. J. 'The inter-disciplinary approach to African History in Nigeria,' *Présence Africaine*, 94, 1975, pp. 171–183.

MCCALL, D. F. *Africa in time-perspective: a discussion of historical reconstruction from unwritten sources*, Legon and Boston, 1964.

VANSINA, JAN, *Oral tradition: a study in historical methodology* (translated by H. M. Wright), Chicago, 1965.

The Uses of Oral Traditions in the Writing of African History

Phillips Stevens, Jr.

In spite of refinements in the applicability of oral traditions to historical writing, there is still considerable opposition to any reliance upon them. This prejudice is unjustified. Just as conscientious Western historians have gone to great efforts to record historical 'fact' in the immutable form of the written word, so too have many non-literate peoples carefully sought to preserve certain of their own historical traditions by other means. Some forms of oral tradition, to be sure, are subject to gross distortion; but others are protected by regulations so strict as to keep the possibilities for their alteration well within the range tolerated by Western historians. It becomes the job of the historian to discover which elements in oral tradition are reliable as sources of data, which are unreliable, and which can provide clues to the location of reliable sources elsewhere, and this task can be so frustrating as to cause the researcher to reject oral sources altogether. Such total rejection has been all too frequent and, in the case of sub-Saharan Africa, has allowed a vast and rich wealth of historical data to go unrecorded.

This need not have been so. A great measure of patience, and a degree of intuition or 'empathy' not generally condoned by conventional historians, are required; but equipped with these two fundamental assets, the researcher can profitably tap the great well of 'living' data that still remains. For the historian who is willing to make the effort, this article is intended as an introduction to the basic forms of oral tradition and the ways in which they are used in their cultural contexts, the possible causes of distortion of these traditions, and how the historian can best investigate these sources.

Forms of oral tradition

For the reconstruction of history from oral sources I have found it useful to distinguish among four broad forms of oral tradition: myth, legend, song, and popular history. All these forms, it can be noted, fall under the generic heading of 'folklore', but this term is so broadly applicable, including nearly all expressive aspects of culture, as to be of no use to this discussion. I should state that the ways in which I define and apply these terms may not accord precisely with the ways other scholars may use them; and the last term is, to my knowledge, my own coinage. We must also be warned that these are not always neat, mutually exclusive categories. But they constitute a good beginning typology; and, if their limitations are recognised, they can be useful tools for the historian.

Myth. Of these four, myth is often the most reliable form. As we commonly use the term, we tend to dismiss myth as the result of irrational attempts by pre-literate and pre-scientific peoples to make sense of their world. But the historian errs gravely if he treats myth so lightly. The English word derives from the Greek *mythos*, meaning that branch of knowledge which is indisputable, not subject to rational argument—as distinct from *logos*. The researcher must first appreciate this value to the culture which reveres it. Myth is true history. It deals with fundamental realities. It explains the origin of things and why things happen the way they do, and it sets down rules for human behaviour. It is often regarded as having been bequeathed by the gods themselves, most of whom lived earthly lives as culture-founders and heroes, during the 'times of the beginnings'. Hence myth is sacred truth, and is hedged about with taboos against its improper use.

Conducting the most serious business of the year, a titled elder of the Bachama village of Fare delivers the sacred history of Nzeanzo, the paramount god. He stands before the shrine of the god (not pictured), facing East, the direction from which Nzeanzo led his people. He holds a sacred emblem which consists of a bundle of short staves festooned with strips of bark. Around the staves are fastened small iron rings which jingle as he swings the emblem in accompaniment to his chanted words. The emblem is connected with the agricultural cycle, which begins with this ritual. Over the speaker's shoulder is the emblem of his office, a curled sceptre made of hippopotamus hide. Above his left elbow is a brass armlet, also designating his office. Before him stand the sacred emblems of the original clans of Fare and certain other villages; elders of these clans are seated in the background. Next to the emblems is a small calabash of unfiltered guinea-corn beer, which will be used for an offering following completion of the speech. Seated close to the speaker are certain elders of his own clan, one of whom will succeed to his position.

C. K. Meek recorded this speech in the late 1920s, and presents a rough translation of a portion of it in his *Tribal Studies in Northern Nigeria* (1931). The gist of the narrative I recorded in 1970 accords almost precisely with his version.

The Uses of Oral Traditions in the Writing of African History

The form and content of myth are carefully preserved, and the recitation of the sacred narrative is strictly controlled. In most instances the one who recites the myth is a priest or other privileged functionary to whom the sacred history has been entrusted. Safeguards against error or lapse of memory are provided in the form of a number of mnemonic (memory-assisting) devices. The speaker recites the sacred words within hearing of a select audience, including those who will inherit his office, or who will perform for him if he is incapacitated. The myth is recited only at an appointed time, usually during a calendrical ritual. The spot on which the speaker stands, the direction he faces, and the way in which he is dressed or accoutred may have significance to the events he is recounting. All these factors combine to re-create the sacred atmosphere of the times of which the myth speaks. The very presence of the actors in the myth—the gods and heroes—is thus invoked, and error cannot be tolerated.

The sacred narrative itself is often structured in a way to assist the memory. Repetition is the most common mnemonic device. If the myth relates the passage of people from place to place, for example, the words describing their journeyings from one locale to another and thence to the next may be exactly the same; only the place names will differ. Similarly, the conditions leading up to whatever unique events may have occurred at each place may be set down in precisely the same phraseology, and the actual events may be described tersely and perhaps dramatically. Poetic rhythm is another memory device. Recitation may be in the form of a chant, or song, with well-defined metre. The tempo of each metric unit may be marked by metronomic accompaniment, such as by a percussion instrument, or by hand-clapping, or by some other auditory device, to ensure that each verse is completed before the next is begun. By any of these means, considerable effort is made to ensure that the sacred narrative does not vary from one recitation to the next.

Just how myth originates is disputed. Psychologists, anthropologists, folklorists and historians all have theories. But it is generally agreed that many elements in myth have bases in fact. Whatever its structure and the nature of its recitation, its content must be considered seriously by the historiographer.

At this point we should consider *folktale*, a form of oral tradition which may be confused with myth, but which in fact stands in important contradistinction to it. As a literary genre, folktale contains many of the same elements as does myth: it may be set in the same 'times of the beginnings', the same gods and heroes may appear (although the principal actors may be animals), and similar events may be alluded to. Folktale often offers explanations of peculiarities in animal and human behaviour and experience, and it may contain morals and express values worthy of emulation. Moreover, its recitation may appear to be controlled. Only certain persons may tell folktales; but this is because these persons have demonstrated that they are good story-tellers. Folktales are generally told at appointed times; but investigation will reveal that these are times of enforced leisure, or times when sharing in a bit of fantasy will not interfere with completion of tasks necessary to the promotion of the general welfare. But the most important distinction the researcher must recognise is that whereas the veracity of myth is indisputable, and its recitation may be an integral part of those rituals enacted to ensure the smooth maintenance of society, it is totally inconsequential whether or not the folktale is believed; its principal purpose is entertainment. Myth is privileged information; folktales are public property. Finally, although the content of folktales appears to receive authentication by the presence of gods or heroes, it is the episodes, strategies employed by the actors, and the moral lessons that they teach, that are important, and not the historical veracity of the details. Moreover, these episodes, strategies, and moral lessons tend to become standardised, so that, by the substitution of recognisable personnel, and by adaptation of events to the appropriate ecological setting, they can speak to all people at all times. Folktale is rarely a reliable source of primary data for the historiographer in Africa.

Legend. This is a specific type of historical narrative that speaks of times since 'the beginnings', after the original culture-founders had departed their earthly lives to assume positions of spiritual advisers, leaving the actual running of society in human control. The whole account derives some authentication by its association with personages, events, or places whose historicity is vouched for in other traditions, but the details of the events described are of questionable historical veracity. Like myth, it deals with real personages (not animals) and real places; like folktale, it lacks divine sanctions and is open to public reference. But unlike both myth and folktale, the details of legend are subject to rational questioning, even by those to whom the account has special significance.

Legend is especially subject to certain processes of alteration and embellishment, which will be discussed shortly. But, by definition, legend has some basis in actual fact, either in terms of its broad framework or by reference to specific names, events, and places. If used carefully, it can be a valuable data source.

Song. This category includes poetry, epic, chant, and other verse forms which are not subject to restrictions of the sort which govern myth. Songs are records of the times, but they can be more. In most instances their composers are relatively free to include statements of social criticism. From such sentiments the historian can reconstruct at least fragmentary pictures of the actual social conditions of the times, and of people's perceptions of and responses to these conditions. Thus song can provide him with the opportunity to bring to historical writing a vitality, an aliveness, that is so often lacking in accounts deriving from more conservative sources.

Song is an often-used vehicle for recording certain special events, such as memorable battles, successful hunts, and the accomplishments of important individuals. Some songs are quite old, especially those composed in praise of royal personages, warrior-heroes, etc. These will be retained and sung periodically, often by persons to whom this function is designated as a special duty, and they may be preserved as carefully as myth. But most often songs are useful to the historian only as records of relatively recent events. This is because songs in traditional societies respond to the same public pressures as songs in modern societies: their appeal and social effect weaken, and they have to be replaced. And with the deaths of the elders, the songs popular in their day also die.

In any case, whether old or recent, songs can be reliable sources of data. Because of their wide public exposure, and also because of the strictures imposed by their metre and rhythm, songs are not generally amenable to alteration. But these very strictures may force their referents to be expressed in symbolic forms, or in metaphors or proverbs understandable only in the language of transmission.

Popular history. History has the effect of validating behaviour and perception of the world and one's place in it, and everyone is history-conscious to some degree. But not everyone has access to or can find relevance or current applicability in the three formal categories discussed above. There exists, therefore, a broad and rather amorphous realm of historical tradition which I have labelled 'popular history'. It is often called simply 'tradition' by historians and anthropologists, but this term is inadequate as it fails to distinguish this form from those more structured and formalised traditions. Popular history derives in part from selected elements in myth, legend, and song, and in part from current events. Lacking the restrictions on its use which govern the other categories, and often lacking concrete referents, popular history is extremely malleable, subject to alteration through diffusion, selection, political opinion, and the need to provide validating precedents for aspects of changing human experience. As it reflects changing values and perceptions it is of great utility to the student of social process, but to the historian it can be utterly confounding. But it should not be dismissed before it has been subjected to careful comparative scrutiny for, if nothing else, it can provide useful clues as to where else to search.

Factors in the distortion of tradition

The above forms of oral tradition have been selected for discussion here because of their potential value as sources for the historian; but before he can attempt to utilise them, he must recognise that all of them, to a greater or lesser degree, are subject to processes of distortion. Most of these factors are discoverable (indeed, many may be universal), and they can be controlled. I shall discuss, and offer brief illustrations of, a few of the most general of such causes of distortion.

Political considerations. We have mentioned the validating effect of history. Having recorded a particular tradition, the historian must first ask, 'What does this tradition *do* for the people who hold it?' He may find that such-and-such a tradition serves to validate the claim of an individual or group to a particular status or degree of social recognition. It may well be that such status was conferred because of such a tradition, hence it does not necessarily follow that the tradition was 'invented' for this purpose. But the historian must be aware that it may have been at least selectively altered to support a particular political aspiration. For example, if the kings of the various Yoruba states could claim direct descent from Odùduwà, the culture founder who established the city of Ifẹ, or if peoples could plausibly claim to have resided in, or even just passed through, Ifẹ during their migrations to their present locations, they could thereby gain significant elevation of social and political status. Most Ifẹ tradi-

The Oba of Lagos wearing a beaded crown

tions assert that only seven kings are entitled to wear the beaded crowns symbolic of divinely-sanctioned authority; but the number of local traditions which assert that their chiefs have such rights, either through direct descent or by some early association, probably cannot be counted.

Alteration of traditions can provide the bases for elevation of an entire society *vis-à-vis* another. The introduction of new values by an expansionist society which is perceived by the indigenes as technologically, or at least militarily, superior, may effect alterations in the natives' traditions; even the sacred myths may reflect some distortion. Thus, in the nineteenth century and probably much earlier, historical accounts of many southern Sudanic peoples were altered so that, for example, migration routes begin in Mecca, in obvious response to the introduction of Islam through the trans-Saharan trade. And it can be seen that some of those who were converted to Islam justified such conversion by adoption of the notion of descent from Muhammad: the traditions of those who were not converted, but who felt threatened by the carriers of Islam, may have been distorted to assert that their forefathers resided peacefully in Mecca or elsewhere in Arabia, but were obliged to flee *to avoid* conversion. Similarly, around the turn of this century the idea of Egyptian origins—strengthened, as we shall see, by the actual writings of historians—became popular, and traditions were distorted to reflect the new ideas that nobility of status could be achieved and maintained only through claims to Egyptian or other Eastern ancestry.

The biological analogy of 'protective colouring' can be appropriate to explain alteration of tradition to express the socially desired feeling of *equality* with certain other peoples. It seems likely that in this way the well-known Kisra legend became established in certain southern Sudanic societies, such as Borgu and Kebbi, both of whom were for a long time threatened, but never conquered, by the great military power of Songhai, where the Kisra tradition already existed. And in this way elements in the popular history of the Bachama, a small kingdom along the upper Benue river, seem to have been altered to assert that—contrary to all linguistic and cultural evidence—the people originated in Sokoto (which they left to avoid conversion to Islam), the campaign headquarters of the *jihad* conducted by the Muslim Fulani who threatened, but never conquered, the Bachama throughout the nineteenth century. Assertion of a Sokoto origin served both as a plea to the Fulani (i.e., 'leave us alone, we too came from there') and as a justification to the people themselves for their continued independence from the Fulani, who were clearly superior militarily.

And finally, traditions may be adapted to express the recognised *inferiority* of one group to another. Until recently the Hutu and Twa of Rwanda justified their positions of servility to the Tuutsi by reference to myths which recount their descent from slaves. But with the current move towards a more egalitarian society, elements in myth and legend which suggest equality have been selected.

And so traditions, especially popular history, may be adapted to express socially and politically convenient sentiments of superiority, equality, or even inferiority, and the historian must be aware of factors which can cause such distortion.

The collapsing of chronology. Analysis of a narrative from its beginning through its subsequent episodes may expose an apparent paradox to the chronology-minded historian. Often, as we have seen, a tradition begins with some wondrous event widely established in popular history. But that initial event may be succeeded by an improbably vast gap in time or geographical distance before the next recorded episode, after which events can happen in rapid-fire succession. Thus, for example, the account of the journey of Kisra from Arabia across the Sahara to the Niger, a distance of some 2500 miles (4000 km), is totally void of details. And the period from the death of Kisra in the seventh century (the date having been ascertained from Arabic documents), to the time of the establishing of various riverine states by his 'sons' some nine or ten centuries later, is totally collapsed in the legend. And those traditions which place Bachama origins in Sokoto do not mention anything that transpired on the 750-mile (1200 km) journey from that city to a place north of the upper Benue river where most of the traditions pick up again, and continue in careful detail. The existence of the initial precipitating event may make the tradition seem older than it could actually be; but the fact that subsequent events may be condensed and collapsed against one another can make those events seem *more recent* than they actually were. This problem illustrates a factor of distortion which is common to oral traditions everywhere: the collapsing of chronology, or what I like to call 'the accordion effect'.

It is a fact of human memory that rarely are events chronicled in specific detail for more than four generations. This is particularly so in African societies, in which the names and achievements of specific ancestors may be remembered, but over succeeding generations specific ancestral events tend to blend into the amorphous—and timeless—realm of 'the ancestors'. And so it is with orally-transmitted traditions. Even the careful and officially-sanctioned preservation of king-lists, and the achievements of each entrant, can succumb to 'the accordion effect'. History is accretionary, but the human mind is selective. Generally speaking, earlier events are collapsed more than recent ones, and this may be a good rule-of-thumb; but the historian must look to the other factors of distortion herein discussed to ascertain why some events are preserved in detail, while others are collapsed. In any case, he must recognise that, in dealing with oral data, his desire to reconstruct accurate chronologies must be greatly tempered.

'*Becoming larger than life*'. Hero-stories in particular illustrate another factor of distortion which is very probably universal: the process of 'becoming larger than life'. Legend, primarily because of its relative freedom from restriction, is particularly susceptible to this process, although the other forms of oral tradition may illustrate it as well. Heroes are, by definition, already somewhat larger than life; but the remembrance of heroes (and anti-heroes) tends to make them more so. The often concomitant infusion of the tales with magical elements, and the attribution of superhuman powers to the heroes themselves, may cause the historian to reject the whole account, rather than to investigate the possibility that the principal actors may have been historical personages. One example from my own research will suffice to illustrate.

Several societies in Adamawa revere the memory of Makwada, a great warrior-hero credited by the Bachama, Bata, Mbula, Kona Jukun, and other groups with having directed certain military successes over the Fulani in the mid-nineteenth century. The Fulani, too, remember him. He is mentioned in European accounts as having sought to persuade the 1854 expedition of W. B. Baikie to assist him in his efforts against the Fulani. He has several lineal descendants now resident in Bachama and Bata villages. But over just a few generations the story of his life has developed into a legend, infused with magical elements and with aspects common to hero-tales elsewhere. According to some variants, shortly after he was born Makwada became lost in the bush, where he was reared by spirits. He returned transformed; even his own father was in awe of him. He became a knight-errant, answering calls from far and wide to fight the Fulani. His exploits were aided by numerous magical stratagems. He could not be killed by weapons of human manufacture. Finally he determined that he would be of greater use to his people as a spirit, and so he instructed a group of his adversaries how to kill him.

So incredible are the exploits of Makwada as recounted in the legend that they can obscure the fact that *he is an historical figure*. Indeed, I was able to use certain elements in the Bachama and Bata versions to corroborate aspects in legend and popular history elsewhere; these helped me to reconstruct portions of the history of the area in the nineteenth century, a period of great intersocietal disruption. But I could not have done so had I not been aware of the processes involved in the development of the legend, and of the necessity for patient comparative research.

The effect of historical writing. Probably the least recognised, but possibly the strongest, factor in the distortion of historical tradition is the effect of written documents. The historian in Africa cannot be advised strongly enough of the power of language. Africans, as most peoples, have a healthy respect for the power of the spoken word (hence the highly-developed art of speaking in proverbs); but once the word has been reduced to writing it acquires an awesome permanence, immutably fixing the events of which it speaks. And oral traditions can be quickly and drastically altered to conform to written history. My informants often attested to the veracity of traditions they had recounted by saying, 'Is it not so written?', referring to a government *Gazetteer* or some other locally-available document. The recently fashionable idea of an Egyptian origin of Yoruba culture was strongly bolstered by Lucas' *Religion of the Yorubas*, and Yoruba traditions are often corroborated by reference to Johnson's famous *History*. Careful historical research has recently suggested that the Nupe legend of the culture-hero Tsoede owes its form solely to its reconstruction in Nadel's *A Black Byzantium*. And some of the informants from whom I obtained the legend of Makwada attested to its historicity by referring me to *The Yola Gazetteer* (1927), wherein portions of it are written.

And so the historian must be twice-warned: he should expect that published works may have had strong effects on the structure and content of the oral traditions he is using; but more important, he should recognise that he himself may be an agent in the distortion of historical tradition, through the release of his published interpretations and conclusions.

Conclusion: the job of the historian

From the foregoing discussion we can enumerate four basic tasks facing the historian who would utilise oral traditions in the reconstruction of African history. First, he should know the *nature* of the form with which he is dealing. Its nature cannot be understood simply by the application of one or another of the labels set down in the first section of this paper; the best guide for the researcher is *how the tradition is treated*, i.e. what regulations, if any, control its use and shape its structure, and how strict are these regulations. Secondly, he must search for factors, both within the society and beyond it, which may have acted to distort the tradition, and he should understand the nature of these factors.

The Uses of Oral Traditions in the Writing of African History

Thirdly, he can consult anthropological method; he should recognise that a tradition has developed *within a particular cultural context* and hence it may be meaningless if considered separate from that context. Further, the tradition may be expressed in, and expressive of, certain symbolic forms understandable only within that culture. The vehicle of such expression is language; the historian thus must be extremely cautious in working through translations, even through the use of a *lingua franca*. And finally, he must use oral traditions as *guides for comparative research*. Elements in traditions must be cross-checked, with other traditions, with anthropological studies, with archaeological data, with the results of linguistic methods such as glotto-chronology, and with written records. It is not an easy job. But with patience and care and the ability to transcend his own cultural and educational biases, the historian in Africa can make good use of oral traditions.

For further reading

BIEBUYCK, D. AND MATEENE, K. C. eds., *The Mwindo Epic from the Banyanga (Congo Republic)*, Berkeley, 1971.

BIOBAKU, S. O. *Sources of Yoruba History*, O.U.P., 1973.

CURTIN, P. D., 'Oral Traditions and African History', *Journal of the Folklore Institute*, vi, 2/3, 1969, pp. 137–155.

FINNEGAN, RUTH, *Oral Literature in Africa*, O.U.P., 1970.

HERSKOVITS, M. J. AND HERSKOVITS, F. S. *Dahomean Narrative: A Cross-Cultural Analysis*, Evanston, 1958.

LAW, R. C. C., 'The Heritage of Oduduwa: Traditional History and Political Propaganda among the Yoruba', *Journal of African History*, xiv, 2, 1973, pp. 207–222.

LOW, V. N., *Three Nigerian Emirates: A Study in Oral History*, Evanston, 1972.

MASON, M., 'The Tsoede Myth and the Nupe Kinglists: More Political Propaganda?', *History in Africa*, II, 1975, pp. 101–111.

STEVENS, P., JR., 'The Kisra Legend and the Distortion of Historical Tradition', *Journal of African History*, xvi, 2, 1975, pp. 185–200.

VANSINA, J., *Oral Tradition: A Study in Historical Methodology*, Chicago, 1965.

Monocausal Explanations In African History: A Prevalent Distortion

A. E. Afigbo

Monocausal explanation in history can be defined simply as the explanation of a historical event or situation in terms *only* or *mainly* of a single factor (or cause), whether that factor is material, spiritual or elemental. The fact is that history, meaning the study of the past activity and experience of man, poses many intractable problems, among which is how to give meaning and significance to an infinite variety of events. Of these events many happen at the same time, while many more follow hot on the heels of those that preceded them a moment earlier and so on into the uncertain present and the speculative future. To record all the events that ever happened in history is beyond human ability, since no mind can possibly comprehend even all the events that took place at any one moment in a given society. Even if such an exercise were possible, it would be merely pointless as it would not make any meaning or explain anything.

As a way out of their dilemma, historians resort to a number of ruses. First they study, for the most part, particular societies rather than just the amorphous phenomenon known as human society. Second, even for a given society, historians tend to concentrate on particular periods, rather than attempting the study of any society in question from the beginning of time—a mind-boggling problem. Third, within a chosen time-span different historians at times concentrate on different episodes or institutions. This detailed demarcation of what would otherwise be a featureless boundless landscape is only a preparation for the historian's most important task—the construction of a story or pattern out of the apparently disparate events, ideas and attitudes which form the constituent elements of an episode such as the slave trade, for example, or of an institution such as slavery.

At the foundation of each story or pattern is the assumption or belief that there must be a manner in which the events which make up an episode are related one to the other. Historiography is the identification of these relationships, the determination of their nature and mode of operation. One of the relationships of events which historians are most prone to identifying and describing is the causal one—the relationship in which it is assumed that few events come about without cause and that few take place without in turn bringing about the occurrence of one or more other events. The historian's preoccupation with causal relationships is part of an attempt to make possible our understanding of the world of reality by means of a system or systems in which the time dimension is fundamental. Each system aims at making reality understandable by a process of simplification. Yet paradoxically not all such systems are simple by themselves. Some are indeed quite complex. However, of all systems of causal explanations known to the historian, the monocausal explanation is the simplest and probably the most primitive in the sense of being the earliest known to man. One or two examples of the early archetypes of the monocausal explanation can be given here.

Modern science seeks to explain the origin and early history of the world in terms of evolutionary changes which took place during billions of years and involved complex chemical and biochemical reactions, some of which were of cataclysmic dimensions. But before the triumph of modern science, man explained these same events in terms of single-factor causation. The Jews, for instance, explained the evolution of the physical universe and of human societies and cultures in terms of a fiat uttered by their supreme God Yahweh. They went further and telescoped the entire history of the world up to the emergence of settled societies into the happenings of a mere seven-day week. Nearer home here in Africa, different peoples had their own versions of this would-be early history of the world told solely in terms of the dynamic intervention of their own local gods. The Edo, for instance, gave it out that their world was brought into being by their high god, *Osanobua*, who peopled it initially with his seven sons whose descendants constitute many of today's ruling dynasties in Nigeria and in 'the land of the white man.'

This simple monocausal explanation of history in terms of the decisive intervention of the Supreme Being in human affairs was not limited to accounts of the origin and development of the world up to the emergence of settled societies. It continued to be used in the explanation of the changing fortunes of the settled societies themselves. To the Jews the God whose fiat brought the world into being in seven days continued to direct their affairs. His pleasure with them was the sole explanation for their prosperity and success in war, while his displeasure was used to account for every tribulation that befell them, including defeat at the hands of enemies who enjoyed military superiority over them. The Christian church in time inherited this tradition, making the supreme God and His Son the prime mover of human destiny, the Lord of a history that has been moving from a definite beginning to an equally definite, if also remorseless, end.

In Africa, especially in non-Islamised Africa, the high god became, after the creation of the world and the emergence of settled societies, a *deus absconditus*, or withdrawn god. Thus, he played very little part in the direction of human history after the conclusion of the creative process. Yet the supernatural remained for the Africans a dominant element in historical causation and was often considered the sole cause of complex events in human society. With Islamised Africa the story was slightly different. The Supreme God, Allah, not just a vague or multifarious supernatural being, remained dominant in human affairs. He 'gave' victory to his faithful servants like Mai Idris Alooma of Borno, while He 'visited' the enemies of His followers (such enemies as the Bulala) with defeats and disasters. Similarly He 'caused' the empires of Songhay and Borno to decay because members of the ruling class had become immoral and base. However, we shall concern ourselves here mainly with monocausal explanations of African history which place the emphasis on the intervention not of extra-historical forces (such as Supreme Gods etc.) but of the human agency

Monocausal Explanations In African History: A Prevalent Distortion

which modern historiography regards as the supreme historical force.

The earliest sustained attempt at the explanation of the historical development of Africa to come down to us was made by Muslim scholars whose activities began to impinge on African societies during the golden age of Arab expansion. The Arab adventurers, soldiers and traders who began penetrating the interior of Africa from about the eighth century A.D. were, like all imperialists, supremely confident of themselves and their culture. Convinced that the world was created in and around their homeland and armed with an arrogantly monotheistic religious ideology, they assumed that 'light and civilisation' spread from the land of their birth to other parts of the world. Reinforcing this belief was their equally dismal ignorance of the history of Africa previous to their advent.

With single-minded devotion and some success they spread this idea whereever they went, embodying it in books of history and religion which their African converts regarded with great awe—thanks to the prestige which attached and still attaches among African peoples to the art of writing. So influential was this idea that man and civilised culture originated in the Middle East and from there migrated to Africa, that many African peoples who came into contact with these missionaries of Islam and the Arab way of life began adjusting their pre-Muslim historical traditions to agree with the historical myth created by Muslim scholars. In this way the Arab or the oriental cause-agent became the most, if not the only important explanation for historical processes in those parts of Africa where Islam and Arab economic interest found a secure foothold. These areas included North Africa, the Sudanic belt stretching from the Atlantic to the Red Sea, and the coast of East Africa.

Wherever this attempt to equate the dominant historical cause-agent with the oriental man gained acceptance among the indigenous elite, it squeezed out of existence other cause-agents and along with them nearly all meaningful references to earlier historical events and accounts. One example of this development can be given from the Central Sudan, or, to be more specific, from Borno. The surviving documents, accounts and traditions relating the early times of the peoples of Borno and the Chad region all suggest that the only significant portion of their history began with the invasion of the area by a certain Arab hero called Saif ibn Dhi Yazan. He is portrayed as having conquered the region and introduced the art of state formation, government and therefore of ordered progress. Of the many changes which must have taken place in the societies of this zone before this purported invasion or migration (which is dated to about the ninth century), we are told next to nothing by these documents. The main impression from these sources is the existence in the area of more or less formless masses of population whose lives moved in no particular direction until this providential conquest by Saif ibn Dhi Yazan and his followers. We are not only told by these sources that meaningful history dawned on the societies of the Chad region only with this conquest, but also that continued change and development in the area depended mainly, if not wholly, on the maintenance of contact with the Arab world. If we had the space we could also show a similar idea being used in the explanation of the history of Hausaland, this time in terms of what is considered to have been the equally providential migration there of Abu Yezid of Baghdad and his followers.

From this monocausal explanation of the political and cultural history of large areas of the central Sudan in terms of the dominant influence of the oriental (Arab) historical cause-agent, all kinds of distortions crept into the historiography of the societies of the Sudanese Zone. For example, as part of the undignified effort to associate themselves with the supposed Arab makers of history, many of the leading families there began to construct fictitious genealogies 'proving' that they descended from prominent Arab lineages in Mecca, Medina or elsewhere. Even certain clans of the Fulani, a people who probably originated in and around the Senegal valley, have with the same ease synthesised for themselves Arab ancestries linking them directly with the Prophet. The same process has been observed among a number of well-placed families in the Swahili society of the East African coast.

The propagation of this idea of the Arab as the dominant historical cause-agent in African history laid the foundation for the most pervasive monocausal explanation of African history. By this I mean that it prepared the ground for the use until recently of *race* as the most, if not the only, important explanation of African historical development.

The nineteenth century, when Europe undertook the effective penetration of the African interior, was also marked by the first large-scale effort to collect historical and ethnographic information about Africa. Unfortunately this was also the time when the theory that *race* was the primary causative factor in history enjoyed widespread currency. In the words of Dr Robert Knox, the Edinburgh anatomist:

> Race is everything; literature, science, art—in a word, civilization depends on it.

Equipped with this view, European travellers and ethnographers in Africa went on avidly collecting all such data as seemed to support their pet theory. In time, and with the aid of all these data, the earlier idea propagated by the Arab historiographical tradition was given further 'refinement'.

Much as the Arabs were prepared to claim all or most of the credit for every significant historical development in those parts of the African interior where they were active, it is not quite certain that they went so far as to assert that wherever their influence was not felt darkness reigned. Their concern was to link such political, economic and social events as impressed them with influences radiated or supposedly radiated by them. But their latter-day European disciples in the racial explanation of African history went further. In the first place, in pressing their own claim to having contributed to the historical evolution of Africa, they argued that the historical cause-agent in Africa was not just the Arab, but the white, otherwise known as the Caucasoid, race. Included in this branch of the human family are the Indo-Europeans, the Semitic-speaking Arabs and the Hamitic-speaking early Egyptians. This broadening of the base of the historical-cause agent made it easier, it was thought, to explain most, if not all important developments in the history of Africa in terms of the single factor of *race*. With this development it could be claimed that what light and civilisation obtained in pre-Islamic Africa 'radiated' from Ancient Egypt. With the eclipse of Egypt and the rise of Islam the Arabs 'took over' the political and cultural education of Africa. For some reason the Arabs soon lost their missionary zeal, or rather the political and military base of their influence soon waned, hence their impact did not embrace all parts of the African continent. From the middle of the nineteenth century, Europe took over the initiative. Between *c*. 1500 and *c*. 1850 this impact was confined to the coasts of West, South-West, South and East Africa. But from about 1850 it embraced the entire continent. Thus, Europe's role in Africa, it was claimed, saw the Caucasoid civilising mission in Africa attain its apogee.

Apart from broadening the base of the historical cause-agent in Africa from the Semitic to the Caucasoid impact, Europe added another dimension to the monocausal explanation of African history in terms of race. Here we refer to the fact that her scholars were not satisfied with merely claiming for the Caucasoid race the credit for all political, social, economic and artistic advance in Africa; on the contrary, they went further. Where institutions and developments which they were prepared to characterise as civilised were absent, they explained this absence by the claim that the Negro did not as a race have the capacity to invent anything culturally significant. In this way *race*, that is, Caucasoid racial genius and the Negro's supposed cultural sterility as a race, came to provide an all-embracing explanation of African history.

One other variant of this Caucasoid-centred explanation of our history must be mentioned briefly here before we go on to discuss its impact on the way our history has been written in this century. The years from *c*. 1840 to *c*. 1885 in West Africa could be described as the golden age of the first generation of our Western-educated elite. This class was made up, for the most part, of those whom the British Anti-Slavery Squadron had recaptured from European slavers and landed in Sierra Leone where they were given a rather stiff dose of education in Western culture. There were, however, other members of the group who had returned to West Africa from either Brazil or North America or the West Indies. These men were greatly impressed by the development gap between Europe and Africa and anxious to close it in the shortest possible time. To this end they sought for the key that would unlock the secret of European progress so as to transfer it to Africa. This most of them found in Christianity and Christianity alone. One of these men, writing in the *Lagos Times* of 9 August 1882, said: 'We know that England and indeed Europe owes her prosperity, greatness and security to Christianity'. In his latest analysis of the ideas and performance of this group Professor E. A. Ayandele has written:

> For the *Saro* this religion (Christianity) was the *primum mobile* of all true progress, the harbinger of material wealth, technological triumphs, national greatness, industrialisation, peace and prosperity ... Among the Egba the educated elite boasted, only the Christian won wars.

Monocausal Explanations In African History: A Prevalent Distortion

With such ideas, many members of the group felt that for Africa to develop rapidly and along the right lines she must be Christianised.

Some other members of this group, people like Edward W. Blyden, who were not so rhapsodic in their appreciation of Christianity, advocated the Islamisation of Africa instead. The two programmes, however, came to the same thing. Advocacy of civilisation through Islamisation was a return to the earlier and narrower idea of the Arab as the important causative agent in African history. The belief that only Christianity civilises re-echoed the later and broader European idea of the Caucasoid racial group as the cultural educator of Africa. Christianity, like Islam, was the ideological invention of the Semitic-speaking peoples but, unlike Islam, was subsequently embroidered by the Europeans. In the context of the time when culture was believed to be racially determined, the belief of our first generation of educated elite in either Christianity or Islam as the beacon that would lead Africa into the new millennium was a subtle way of subscribing to the monocausal racial explanation of our destiny sketched above.

This monocausal explanation of African history in terms of race has had a far-reaching impact on African historical writing. And in spite of the fact that African historians have attacked it vehemently and consistently from about the 1950s, its influence continues to be felt in different ways. In the period of colonial rule, it provided part of the convenient ideological justification for all kinds of policies. For instance, it provided one of the arguments for the great efforts made by the British in Northern Nigeria and elsewhere to uphold the claims of certain ethnic nationalities and political classes to political rulership. The Fulani emirs of Northern Nigeria were widely described as born rulers of men because they were wrongly believed to be a branch of the Caucasoid racial stock which was said to have been responsible for the political education of Africa. Elsewhere, for instance in Benin, Yorubaland and Asante, the political and/or economic elite whom the British overthrew and sought to use at different levels of the administrative system were believed (for example, by colonial officials such as Herbert Palmer) to derive, however remotely, from the same racial stock.

With the dawn of nationalist politics, however, especially with the massive spread of Western education among peoples who were despised because they were believed to comprise largely pure Negro stock, the idea that political ability varies directly according to the degree of Caucasoid racial impact came to be seriously shaken.

If this theory of racial causation in African history no longer informs practical politics or no longer constitutes an essential ingredient of political belief, it continues to show much capacity for metamorphosis and rebirth in the realm of African historiography. In the 1930s Professor Seligman could describe the civilisation of precolonial Africa as the civilisation of the Hamites because at the time nobody questioned the assumption that the Negro by himself was culturally inert and sterile. By the 1960s, however, the idea had come under fire as important historical movements and cultural developments came to be traced for periods in the African past and in areas of Africa from which the Arab impact

A Fulani Emir

was absent. Yet, writing in 1962, Professors Oliver and Fage went on to explain the political history of Sub-Saharan Africa in terms of the racial impact of the Caucasoids on the Negro. They claimed that the Negro state system, which they characterised as 'Sudanic Civilisation', can be traced to stimuli radiating from Ancient Egypt via the Nile valley.

Even though this restatement of the old myth has also been seriously assailed, it continues to rear its head in different forms. Thus in 1971 Dr A. J. H. Latham explained the evolution of Efik society in the three centuries between 1600 and 1891 in terms only of European commercial impact. On the other hand the Oron clan of the Ibibio, who are located inland from the Efik, were described as having remained static and unchanging during those same centuries simply because their society did not come into direct contact with the stimulus from visiting European traders. In a sense Latham's book takes us back more or less to the nineteenth century when the presence of so-called 'civilised' institutions in any African society was accounted for in terms of Caucasoid impact and their absence in terms of Negro incapacity for initiating change independently.

Most historians recognise that the monocausal explanation of historical situations is a form of distortion. In practice, however, a number of factors at times drive them relentlessly into adopting that very method. One of these is insufficient documentation, as in pre-colonial Africa where most societies were non-literate or nearly so, as a result of which many developments went unrecorded or only partially recorded, at least in the conventional sense. Much of what was recorded dealt with the activities of visiting Arabs and Europeans. Not surprisingly, therefore, a purely documentary approach to the study of African societies in this period has tended to end in the investigation of changes induced or supposedly induced by Arabs and Europeans. We are gradually moving away from this Arab and European-centred interpretation of our history through supplementing the surviving conventional documents with evidence from oral tradition, archaeology and linguistics. These show that other forces were operative in African society along with, and at times in place of, the Arab or European visitor.

There is another factor which also appears to drive historians towards the adoption of monocausal explanation. This is ideological commitment. Those who seek to explain history in terms of the working of a divine idea are usually devout men like the Old Testament prophets or St Augustine of Hippo. It is understandable that they should want to use man's historical experience to drive home the message of the overriding will and power of God. The same is true of those who seek to account for historical change in terms only of economic forces—or, as they put it, in terms of changes in the mode and structure of production. These latter are committed to Marxism which they see as the ultimate solution to the problems of organising a just and equitable human society. The impact of historians of this school in the field of African history is just beginning to be felt. Their most compendious work so far in this area is Endre Sik's account of African history from earliest times to independence using the monocausal Marxist line. In some respects the explanation of African history in terms of race and race alone, discussed above, falls into this category of commitment to ideology—this time race ideology.

There is yet a third factor—the quest by historians for simple explanations of complex human situations. We have already drawn attention to the fact that it is only by means of some system of explanation that we can impose order and meaning on the innumerable events which go to make up human experience. This quest for simplicity in explanation is often combined with the belief that a historian should, as much as possible, abstract from a total historical situation a factor which he considers as holding the key to our understanding of what actually happened. This factor he is expected to play up as his own special discovery, his own contribution to the continuing debate. It is this quest which helps one to understand why Professor K. O. Dike thought that 'the history of modern West Africa is largely the history of five centuries of trade with European nations', thus subordinating all else that happened in West Africa in those centuries to the European impact which during the period did not in fact penetrate more than a few miles beyond the coast.

One recognises, as an eminent English historian has said, that there is no democratic principle in history according to which all facts are equal. One must therefore distinguish between important and unimportant facts, between dominant and subordinate causative factors. But in doing so we must bear steadily in mind the need not to distort reality by either over-simplifying or over-dramatising it.

For further reading

AFIGBO, A. E. 'Monocausality and African Historiography: The Case of Efik Society and International Commerce, *Transactions of the Historical Society of Ghana*, xiv, 1, pp. 117–127.

—— 'Herbert Richmond Palmer and Indirect Rule in Eastern Nigeria 1915–1928', *Journal of the Historical Society of Nigeria*, iii, 2, 1965, pp. 295–312.

AYANDELE, E. A. *The Educated Elite in the Nigerian Society*, I.U.P., 1974.

BOHANNAN, P. AND CURTIN, P., *Africa and Africans*, New York, 1971.

DIKE, K. O., *Trade and Politics in the Niger Delta*, O.U.P. 1956.

DIKE, K. O. AND AJAYI, J. F. A., 'African Historiography', *International Encyclopaedia of Social Sciences*, The Macmillan Company and the Free Press of Glencoe, 1968, vol. 6, pp. 394–400.

HODGKIN, T., *Nigerian Perspectives*, O.U.P., 1975, second edition.

LATHAM, A. J. H., *Old Calabar 1600–1891*, O.U.P., 1973.

MURDOCK, G. P., *Africa: Its Peoples and Their Culture History*, New York, 1959.

OLIVER, R. AND FAGE, J. D., *A Short History of Africa,* Penguin, 1962.

SELIGMAN, C. G., *Races of Africa*, H.U.L., 3rd edition, 1957.

The Marxist Approach to Historical Explanation

Robin Law

Marx and 'Marxism'

'Marxism' is a convenient label for that body of thought which derives from the work of Karl Marx (1818–1883) and his close collaborator Friedrich Engels (1820–1895). But it must be stressed at the outset that 'Marxism' does not constitute a unified body of thought, and that there is no single 'Marxist' position but rather a number of rival views which can all claim to be 'Marxist' in the sense of sharing certain assumptions and methodological approaches originally enunciated by Marx. Marx and Engels themselves changed their views, at least in detail and emphasis, in the successive works which they wrote between the 1840s and the 1890s, and there are also significant differences of emphasis (and, it is sometimes claimed, some major differences of substance) between Marx and Engels. Some later 'Marxist' thinkers certainly developed views which would have been repudiated by Marx and Engels: indeed, even during Marx's own lifetime, he found it necessary to dissociate himself from certain of his followers, declaring 'All I know is that I am not a Marxist'. From the 1890s, 'Marxists' became divided into a number of mutually hostile factions, each claiming to represent 'orthodox' Marxist theory: the faction associated with the Russian Communist Party, which derives its theories mainly from the work of V. I. Lenin (1870–1924), has been politically the most important, but from the point of view of theory it represents only one variant of 'Marxism' among several. In the present article, there is clearly not enough space for a survey of all the various 'Marxist' theories of history, and attention is therefore restricted to the views of Marx and Engels themselves. It should not be supposed, however, that the writings of Marx and Engels anywhere contain a final and definitive statement of the orthodox 'Marxist' position: Marx and Engels themselves always regarded their writings as no more than an approximation, which would necessarily be modified in the light of future research.

Although 'Marxist' theory is concerned with much more than the interpretation of history, a particular approach to historical explanation has always been central to it. This approach has commonly been known as 'the materialist conception of history' or as 'historical materialism', two labels which were invented by Engels and were never in fact used by Marx himself. (The alternative labels, 'the economic interpretation of history' and 'dialectical materialism', were invented by subsequent Marxist writers.) Marx and Engels first worked out their conception of history in a joint work, *The German Ideology*, written in 1845–6. What is usually regarded as the classic formulation of their views is that included by Marx in the Preface of his *Contribution to the Critique of Political Economy*, published in 1859. A third influential exposition is

Karl Marx

Freidrich Engels

V. I. Lenin

that offered by Engels in his work *Anti-Dühring*, published in 1878. After Marx's death, Engels was also responsible for an important attempt to reformulate the Marxist conception of history, in the light of criticism of it, in letters written in 1890–4[1]. It is these works which form the basis for the account which follows.

The Marxist model

The Marxist model of the historical process is perhaps best summarised in the words of Marx himself, in the classic formulation which he wrote in 1859:

> In the social production of their life, men enter into definite relations that are indispensable and independent of their will, relations of production which correspond to a definite stage of development of their material productive forces. The sum total of these relations of production constitutes the economic structure of society, the real foundation, on which rises a legal and political superstructure and to which correspond definite forms of social consciousness. The mode of production of material life conditions the social, political and intellectual life process in general. It is not the consciousness of men that determines their being, but, on the contrary, their social being that determines their consciousness. At a certain stage of their development, the material productive forces of society come into conflict with the existing relations of production, or—what is but a legal expression for the same thing— with the property relations within which they have been at work hitherto. From forms of development of the productive forces these relations turn into their fetters. Then begins an epoch of social revolution. With the change of the economic foundation the entire immense superstructure is more or less rapidly transformed. In considering such transformations a distinction should always be made between the material transformation of the economic conditions of production, which can be determined with the precision of natural science, and the legal, political, religious, aesthetic or philosophic—in short, ideological forms in which men become conscious of this conflict and fight it out. Just as our opinion of an individual is not based on what he thinks of himself, so can we not judge of such a period of transformation by its own consciousness; on the contrary, this consciousness must be explained rather from the contradictions of material life, from the existing conflict between the social productive forces and the relations of production.

The central point which Marx wishes to make in this passage is that the general character of any society is determined by its 'economic structure', that is, by the manner in which goods are produced. Marx expresses this by means of an architectural metaphor: the economic structure constitutes the 'foundation' (or more commonly, the 'base'), while the political and legal institutions and the dominant ideologies are the 'superstructure' built upon this foundation. The 'economic base' comprises two elements: the 'forces of production' (or 'produc-

---

[1] See especially the letters of Engels to Conrad Schmidt, 5 August 1890; to Joseph Bloch, 21 September 1890; to Conrad Schmidt, 27 October 1890; to Franz Mehring, 14 July 1893; to W. Borgius, 25 January 1894.

tive forces') and the 'relations of production' (together forming the 'mode of production')—the former being the material objects (raw materials and tools) and the labour force employed in the production of goods, the latter being the ways in which men co-operate with one another in order to produce goods. The forces of production and the relations of production are closely connected, since different forces of production evidently require different patterns of co-operation for their exploitation: for example, the introduction of complex machinery necessitates a substantial enlargement of the unit of production and an increasingly specialised division of labour among the workers employed in it. The relations of production in turn determine the character of the legal and political institutions of society, since the legal system gives formal expression to the rules of behaviour needed to maintain the existing economic system and the political system is controlled by those who dominate the process of production and provides the coercive force needed to ensure that the existing economic system is maintained: for example, slavery or serfdom can only be maintained if the legal system guarantees the rights of the slave-owners or landowners and if state power can be employed to protect their position against any threat from the disprivileged. The economic, legal, and political systems in turn determine the character of the dominant ideas, or 'ideology', since ultimately they can only be maintained if they are felt to be right, and it is the dominant ideology which provides this legitimacy by presenting the existing form of society as being in conformity with divine justice, reason, or whatever is the fashionable idiom: for example, ideas of individual liberty serve to legitimise a free market economy.

Marx thus believed that different forms of society were based ultimately on different modes of production. Looking at the history of Europe, he distinguished three major forms of society down to his own day, each based on a different mode of production: first, the 'ancient society' of Classical Greece and the Roman Empire, based upon slavery; second, the 'feudal society' of medieval Europe, based upon serfdom in agriculture and the guild system in manufacturing; and third, the 'capitalist society' which emerged in Europe from the seventeenth century onwards, which was based upon wage labour. (Marx also believed that the capitalist society of his own day would inevitably evolve into a 'socialist society', which would be based upon communal ownership.)

It must be stressed that this schema of successive ancient, feudal, and capitalist societies was intended by Marx to summarise *European* developments, and was not (contrary to a common misconception) presented as a universally applicable law setting out the stages through which *all* human societies must pass: in fact, he specifically objected to the suggestion that the future development of Russia would necessarily replicate the experience of western Europe[2]. Marx and Engels knew little of the non-European world. They did attempt in certain works to sketch a model of an 'Asiatic' form of society, derived mainly from material available on India and China. This 'Asiatic' form

---

[2] See the letter of Marx to the Editorial Board of the *Otechestvenniye Zapiski*, November 1877.

The Marxist Approach to Historical Explanation

The storming of the Bastille during the French revolution, 1789

of society was supposedly based upon a state monopoly of landownership and the undertaking by the state of large-scale public works (especially for irrigation): this form of society was supposed to be essentially unchanging, and Asian societies could only be propelled into the capitalist stage through the impact of European imperialism. However, the quality of the information on Asian societies available to Marx and Engels was poor, and their picture of Asian economic structures was wildly inaccurate, so that their views on the character of 'Asiatic society' are of no more than antiquarian interest. Marx and Engels were totally ignorant of sub-Saharan Africa, and made no attempt to delineate a model of an African 'mode of production'.

Since different forms of society were based upon different 'modes of production', changes from one form of society to another derived from changes in the mode of production, or more specifically from the progressive development of the 'forces of production'. Marx and Engels used the term 'social revolution' to refer to the period during which the transition from one form of society to another was effected. New forces of production can develop for a while within the existing form of society, but eventually a point is reached where their further development is inhibited by the survival of legal, political and ideological structures corresponding to the old mode of production: Marx and Engels used the metaphor of 'contradiction' to refer to this incompatibility between the development of the new forces of production and the maintenance of the 'superstructure' corresponding to the old relations of production. In these circumstances, the outmoded elements of the superstructure have to be swept away in order to permit the further development of the productive forces. In their detailed writings Marx and Engels were mainly concerned with the transition from feudal to capitalist society, and they held that the English Revolution of the 1640s and the French Revolution of 1789 both represented a crucial phase in this 'social revolution', since they destroyed surviving legal structures which were incompatible with the development of capitalism (such as serfdom, guilds, and other restrictions of free enterprise) and overthrew the political dominance of the feudal landowners in favour of the rising capitalist bourgeoisie. (It should be pointed out that this interpretation of the significance of the English and French Revolutions would be strongly challenged by many non-Marxist historians.)

It should by now be clear that (contrary to another popular misconception) Marx and Engels did *not* believe that all human actions are motivated by economic interest. Their theory allows that people's *motives* may be (indeed, usually are) not economic, but holds that there are economic *causes* for the dominance of particular motives: for example, that the dominance of militaristic values (glory, courage, etc.) in particular periods is to be explained by the economic character of these societies. Their theory is not in fact intended to explain the actions of *individuals* at all; it is not indeed primarily concerned with the explanation of individual historical events. What it seeks to explain, and what it claims to explain in economic terms, is the *general character of society*; and further, the general process of *social change*.

The exposition of the Marxist conception of history in Marx's Preface of 1859 is very compressed and highly abstract. In consequence, it contains a number of ambiguities which may give rise to considerable problems when a historian seeks to apply Marx's theory to a particular historical problem. Two major sources of difficulty will be noted here. First, while it is clear that Marx seeks the ultimate cause of social change in the development of the forces of production, it is left extremely unclear how he believed this development of the forces of production itself came about. On the face of it, social change is explained as a consequence of economic change, but economic change is itself left unexplained. In other works, however, especially when dealing with particular historical problems, Marx and Engels do offer a number of observations on the causes of economic change. For example, Marx connects the development of slavery in ancient Greece with the growth of population, which created an increased demand for land and therefore stimulated wars of conquest[3]. In other contexts, particularly with regard to the development of capitalism in Europe, Marx and Engels stressed the importance of the expansion of trade, which led to innovation in the production process in order to meet expanding demand. These and other suggestions of Marx and Engels are plausible enough, but they are admittedly

---

[3] See Marx, *Pre-Capitalist Economic Formations*, edited by E. J. Hobsbawm, Lawrence and Wishart, London, pp. 92–93.

difficult to reconcile with the model sketched out in the 1859 Preface: in particular, their stress on the role of expanding trade seems to suggest that it was change in the relations of production (specifically, in the sphere of exchange) which led to change in the forces of production, rather than *vice versa*. However, the exposition in the 1859 Preface is necessarily, since it is so brief, somewhat oversimplified, and Marx and Engels undoubtedly believed that the explanation of economic change could only be based upon detailed empirical research into each specific historical situation, and should not be imposed upon the evidence in the light of a preconceived theory.

The second difficulty, which is closely related to the first, is that while in the Preface of 1859 and in other general statements of their position, Marx and Engels stress the derivation of legal, political, and ideological developments from changes in the economic structure, they were well aware that in many specific historical contexts this relationship was in fact reversed, and that economic change might be promoted or obstructed by political action or by the prevalence of particular ideas and values. They argued, however, that while political action and ideological developments could slow down or hasten economic development, they could not change the essential direction of this development. Engels, in his letters of the 1890s, conceded that it was only 'ultimately' that economic change determined the course of social change, and that in the short run non-economic factors might well appear to be predominant. It follows that, in the study of any particular historical problem, 'economic determinism' cannot be assumed to be operative, but must be shown to apply (or not to apply) by reference to a detailed analysis of the available evidence. Here again, these qualifications yield a much more complicated picture than that suggested by abbreviated statements such as that in the 1859 Preface, but Marx and Engels were always empiricists and not dogmatists, and their theory was intended merely as a characterisation of a particular approach to the question of historical explanation, and not as a preconceived 'solution' to all specific historical problems.

History as 'class struggle'
The Preface of 1859 contains no reference to social classes or to class struggle; yet in their most famous work, the *Communist Manifesto* of 1848, Marx and Engels had declared that 'the history of all hitherto existing society is the history of class struggles'. The contradiction, however, is only apparent. In the Preface, Marx speaks of the relationship between the 'economic foundation' and the 'superstructure' and between the 'forces of production' and the 'relations of production', and so forth. But terms such as these are merely abstractions, or shorthand ways of referring to the activities of *people*. History, as Marx and Engels well knew, is made not by 'forces', 'factors', or 'principles', but by individual human beings, and historical change is brought about by conflict not between 'structures' or 'systems', but between groups of individual human beings. When, for example, Marx speaks of the 'contradiction' between new forces of production and the existing relations of production, he means a conflict

between one group of people who are developing the new forces of production, and another committed to the maintenance of the old relations of production. Marx and Engels believed, of course, that the most significant and enduring groupings of people were based upon common economic interests, and they referred to these economically based groupings as 'classes'. In stating that 'all history' was 'the history of class struggles', therefore, Marx and Engels were doing no more than reiterating their belief in the determining role of the economic structure, but doing so in a way which incorporates a salutary reminder that it is people, and not abstractions, who are the agents of historical change.

There is, however, an important ambiguity in the Marxist concept of 'class'. Although in many contexts Marx and Engels employ the term 'class' to refer to any grouping of people whose ultimate basis is economic, in other contexts they use it in a more restricted sense, to distinguish those groupings which are not only based upon a common economic interest but are also *conscious* of this economic basis: those groups which, in Marxist jargon, possess 'class-consciousness'. 'Classes' in this narrower sense only emerged, according to Marx and Engels, with the development of the 'bourgeoisie' and 'proletariat' of modern capitalist society: in earlier social formations, although social groupings were *in fact* based ultimately upon economic interests, people were not (or at least, only imperfectly) *conscious* of this. In this narrower sense of 'class', therefore, far from 'all history' being characterised by 'class struggle', the concept of 'class' is fully applicable only to capitalist societies.

'Determinism' and 'historical laws'

It is often supposed that an essential element—or even *the* essential element—in the Marxist conception of history is a belief in 'determinism', that is, the view that whatever happens in history is inevitable, and in the existence of 'historical laws'. (It is perhaps worth noting that these are really two separate issues: it is quite possible to be a 'determinist' without believing in 'historical laws', an example of this being G. W. F. Hegel (1770–1831), a philosopher who had a considerable influence on Marx.) In fact, however, the questions of 'determinism' and of 'historical laws' are really quite peripheral to the central concerns of the Marxist conception of history.

To take first the question of 'determinism': while it is true that Marx and Engels often use words like 'inevitable' and 'necessary' in describing particular historical developments, this is usually little more than a stylistic flourish. Certainly, Marx and Engels did *not* believe that the detailed course of events, as opposed to the general direction of social change, was in any sense inevitably determined. They were quite ready to recognise the role of 'accidents' and of the purposive actions of individual human beings in affecting the course of events. The belief that Marx and Engels were rigid 'determinists' appears to have arisen from the misconception that they regarded people's actions as being determined by 'the economy'. In fact, as noted earlier, 'the economy' is not something separate from human activity, which determines how men act: it *is* how men act.

G. W. F. Hegel

in the process of producing and procuring the goods necessary for sustenance. In stressing the importance of 'the economy', therefore, Marx and Engels were not denying the effectiveness of human action in 'changing the course of history'; they were asserting it.

Equally, Marx and Engels often refer to 'laws' of history, apparently analogous to the laws established by the physical sciences. But here again, this is in many instances no more than a rhetorical conceit. It was certainly not their view that the study of history should be primarily directed towards identifying historical laws, and the reader who searches through their works in the hope of finding such laws will discover that they claimed to have established very few indeed. They believed that it was possible to generalise to some extent about the way in which particular forms of society—such as capitalist societies—were organised, and even that it was possible to predict the future development of capitalist society on the basis of such generalisations. They were well aware, however, that in formulating such 'laws', they were merely summarising, in a necessarily oversimplified form, broadly similar developments in broadly similar societies: 'historical laws' for them were generalisations *abstracted from* particular historical situations, not independent forces which in some sense *determined* the course of events in these particular historical situations. They were also extremely wary of generalisations which purported to be applicable to *all* human societies, believing rather that the different forms of society ('ancient', 'feudal', 'capitalist', and 'Asiatic') each had their own peculiar 'laws'.

Conclusion

In conclusion, it should be stressed that Marx and Engels never intended their theory of history to be a substitute for the detailed work of empirical research. In their earliest exposition of their view of history, in the *German Ideology* of 1845–6, they specifically warned that their theories 'by no means afford a recipe or a schema ... for neatly trimming the epochs of history; on the contrary, our difficulties begin only when we set about the observation and the arrangement—the real depiction—of our historical material'. Their theory was offered as a summary of the conclusions they derived from their own detailed research, and as suggesting a fruitful approach to historical research in the future, but it was always implicit (and sometimes explicit) that their own conclusions might well require revision in the light of future work. Since the 1890s, it has become customary for self-styled 'Marxists' to condemn attempts to modify the conclusions of Marx and Engels as 'revisionism', but in defending the letter of their writings they falsify their spirit: all 'Marxists' should be 'revisionists' as a matter of principle.

For further reading

The most important works of Marx and Engels which deal with their conception of history are the following:

> MARX, KARL AND ENGELS, FRIEDRICH, *The German Ideology*, Part One, edited by C. J. Arthur, Lawrence and Wishart, 1846.
>
> MARX, KARL, *Contribution to the Critique of Political Economy*, Lawrence and Wishart, 1859.
>
> ENGELS, FRIEDRICH, *Anti-Dühring*, Lawrence and Wishart, 1878.
>
> ENGELS, FRIEDRICH, *Ludwig Feuerbach and the End of Classical German Philosophy*, Progress Publishers, Moscow.

Among works by later Marxist writers, the following are perhaps the most useful:

PLEKHANOV, GEORGE, *Fundamental Problems of Marxism*, edited by J. S. Allen, Lawrence and Wishart, 1965.

FLEISCHER, HELMUT, *Marxism and History*, Harper and Row, New York.

For intelligent criticisms of the Marxist conception of history, see e.g.:

ACTON, H. B. *The Illusion of the Epoch*, Routledge and Kegan Paul, 1955.

LEFF, GORDON, *The Tyranny of Concepts*, Merlin Press, 1964.

Historical Explanation: The Heresy of Historicism

Jeremy White

'Historicism' is a term coined to designate two different although related notions. The first is the notion that there are in history certain patterns, trends, or laws, which if discovered can enable the historian to predict the future. According to this notion the task of the historian should consist in a search for general laws, for example laws governing the development of society, in a manner similar to that in which natural scientists search for laws. Thus considered history would be a science. (It should be noted here that the word 'history' also has two different though related meanings. History in its primary sense—as used in the second sentence of this article—means 'the actual course of events'; history in its secondary and derived sense means 'what the historian writes about those events'. 'History' is used in this second sense when it is described as a science or branch of knowledge.)

The second meaning of historicism is summed up in the Latin tag: *Veritas et virtus filiae temporis* (Truth and virtue are daughters of time). In other words truth and moral values are not unchanging and eternal absolutes, but change with time. For instance, slavery, according to the historicist, cannot be adjudged right or wrong, good or bad, in any absolute way; it can only be considered good or bad in relation to the prevailing set of values of the time and place. By this the historicist not only means that the historian should avoid passing judgment on the values of societies different from his own as if his own values were necessarily superior: this would indeed be a very reasonable precept since the historian's primary task is to understand, not to be a judge. The historicist means much more: he means that all moral values are relative, that we can never say that any particular action is absolutely good or absolutely bad. Here in effect the historicist is taking an illegitimate step outside the bounds of history (in its secondary sense) and constituting himself into an authority upon morals or values, a role proper to the philosopher or theologian, not to the historian.

Before going further in this explanation of historicism, it will be as well to give one or two concrete examples of it from writings about Africa. These will help explain why historicism deserves the title of 'heresy', that is, deviation from the truth.

Two examples which show how the two forms of historicism are in practice, as well as in theory, usually closely linked, are: firstly an article by Professor J. D. Fage (in the *Journal of African History*, 1969) called 'Slavery and the Slave Trade in the Context of West African History', and secondly Professor J. D. Omer-Cooper's well known book *The Zulu Aftermath: A Nineteenth-Century Revolution in Bantu Africa* (Longman, 1966). Fage's article is a radical reassessment of the Atlantic slave trade in which he challenges the hitherto generally

Historical Explanation: The Heresy of Historicism

accepted view that this trade did great damage to West African societies both in terms of depopulation and in terms of the political instability it provoked. Fage argues on the one hand that the depopulation caused was far less than originally thought, to the extent that the trade did not much affect West African societies considered as collectivities, and on the other hand that the slave trade in fact contributed to political development in that it helped West African rulers build up strong, centralised states: slavery was the means of 'mobilizing labour for economic and political needs of the state'. Fage's summary of his argument runs as follows:

> On the whole it is probably true to say that the operation of the slave trade may have tended to integrate, strengthen and develop unitary, territorial authority, but to weaken or destroy more segmentary societies. Whether this was good or evil may be a nice point; historically it may be seen as purposive and perhaps as more or less inevitable.

If one puts this passage together with another where Fage speaks of the European powers as 'continuing the process, initiated by African kings and entrepreneurs, of conquering the segmentary societies and absorbing them into unitary political structures' it is easy to spot the presence of the two forms of

The slave trade in West Africa: did it 'contribute to political development'?

historicism. In the first place Fage sees in West African history (the course of events) a 'process' at work which 'more or less inevitabl[y]' and in a 'purposive' way leads West African societies through certain stages towards the goal of the modern twentieth-century nation state. In the second place, despite his apparent effort to avoid passing moral judgment on this process, and in particular on the contribution to it of the slave trade, Fage's use of the word 'purposive' could, in the context of his article as a whole, too easily be taken to indicate moral approval: anything which contributes to the process of state-formation and nation-building is regarded as 'progressive'. But notice that not only does Fage believe some 'purposive process' at work in West African history—one wonders to whom the purpose belonged—but also, even though unconsciously, he appears to be giving moral approval to the slave trade! What most men regard as a moral evil, he calls 'purposive'. He has thus subordinated an absolute and universal moral criterion of good and evil to a merely political criterion and one strictly limited to a particular time and place, namely the criterion of the modern nation state.

It is not, let it be stressed, that Fage's interpretation of the relevant historical evidence is necessarily mistaken, or that there is anything inherently wrong with the modern nation state (as one among many perfectly legitimate forms of political organisation). My objection is rather to his apparent assumption that there is some conscious purpose at work in West African history whose fulfilment is 'more or less inevitable' and therefore, by implication, could be considered either necessarily good, or—since what is inevitable cannot properly be qualified as good or bad—somehow outside and above moral classification. The passage quoted seems to discount the element of human freedom as a factor in history, and also that the goodness or evil of a particular human action—such as a slave raid, for instance—can only be judged in the last analysis against a universal, permanent criterion of right and wrong, not against the fluctuating attitudes of successive periods and societies of history.

The second example is very similar to the first. The relevant passage from Omer-Cooper runs:

> ... all the Zulu-type Kingdoms could be said to constitute experiments in multi-tribal nation-building. One of the most striking features of the *Mfecane* is indeed the very general success which attended the numerous and different attempts at forming political units out of originally separate peoples. It suggests that the task of instilling a sense of political unity into peoples of different language and culture in a limited time, the task which faces every political leader in the newly independent countries, is not so difficult as pessimists tend to maintain.

Here again the author is elevating to the level of an absolute standard and goal a particular form of political organisation popular at the present moment in history in some parts of the world, as if it constituted an ultimate state of perfection towards which all earlier history has been inevitably leading.

Historical Explanation: The Heresy of Historicism

Shaka, Zulu kingdom-builder

Once again the author finds himself making the end justify the means. For, as C. C. Wrigley pointed out in his useful article 'Historicism in Africa' (1971), Omer-Cooper has earlier shown that Shaka, the most 'successful' Zulu kingdom-builder, was 'a raging psychopath' because of whose 'insane ambitions many tens of thousands of people died of violence and starvation'. The career of Shaka, by Omer-Cooper's own account, is one of the last models or examples one would recommend any contemporary leader to try to emulate in 'the task of instilling a sense of political unity into peoples of different language and culture in a limited time'. National unity, like every sort of worthwhile unity among men, cannot be forced upon people, if it is going to last. And it must be built upon a foundation of justice, in virtue of which fundamental human rights such as the right to life and property are respected.

Wrigley suggests that both Fage and Omer-Cooper have been influenced by a historicist trend of thought popular among some anthropologists. He instances Marshall D. Sahlins' three-volume work *The Hunters, Tribesmen,* and *The Formation of States* as a typical influential 'model' of the evolution of society supposedly applicable to African history, according to which society passes through various stages of development, always moving from the more primitive to the more complex and sophisticated, until finally the modern nation state is reached. The model, instead of being kept as a useful servant, that is, as a conceptual instrument which helps one to distinguish clearly between different types of society on the theoretical level, has been allowed to become the master. For the model has eventually been mistaken for reality, for what actually happened.

Now historical research over a wider area than just West Africa, as well as research into the past of West Africa over a longer period than just the last few centuries, in fact shows that the Sahlins model is not an accurate explanation of what happened: it can only fit some areas, and for certain periods of time. That there is nothing inherently either inevitable or universal about such a pattern of societal evolution is shown, for instance, by the discovery that in Bantu Africa the general tendency between the sixteenth and nineteenth centuries seems to have been towards political dispersion, not towards centralisation. Indeed, if there is one thing a wide knowledge of history over long periods of time shows, it is that progress is not inevitable anywhere and, where there is progress, it does not consist of moving along a single, uniform path towards a single uniform goal. Human life is more complex and richer than that, and also more mysterious.

The two examples given of historicism so far show how historicism can affect (or infect) intelligent and humane scholars, probably without their even being aware of it (such is the influence of certain philosophical ideas). A very different case is that of scholars who embrace historicist principles consciously, such as the English historian E. H. Carr, author of a widely-respected *History of Russia*. To this category also belong Marxist writers, although their reasons for embracing historicism are somewhat different.

Carr is a good example of a historian who has confused history with philosophy, with disastrous results both for philosophy and for history. Like the ancient Greek philospher Heraclitus, he is so impressed by the fact of change which he sees going on all around him—for instance, birth and growth, decay and death on the level of living things; corrosion at the level of non-living things—that he is deceived into thinking that everything in reality is in a state of constant flux. Now if this is so, he argues, and if it is precisely the role of history (as a branch of knowledge) to study change—that is, change in general, not only change in human society—it follows that the science (or art) of history must be the supreme science and *ultima magistra vitae* (the ultimate or highest teacher of life). Carr, of course, does not explicitly reason in the way just described. But essentially his mode of thinking can be explained along these lines. In effect he has adopted the (unproved) assumption of many European thinkers in the period following the French Revolution—including Hegel and Marx—that 'the nature of anything is entirely comprehended in its development'. In other words you can only understand something properly if you look at it over the entire period of its development through time. On the surface this view looks quite convincing: you can hardly understand fully the nature of the German people, for instance, as a national group, unless you study their development over the centuries; likewise, the nature of a seed cannot be fully appreciated unless you also study it after it has become a tree. You can add that the historian seldom likes to commit himself to a judgment upon the career of a living person, precisely because that person is still in a process of development; a complete picture of him cannot be achieved until he is dead.

On the other hand, if you look more closely—particularly at the last two examples—you will appreciate that while there is obviously a difference between the seed and the tree it becomes later, and between the baby Napoleon and the Emperor Napoleon, there is also in each case something the same, something which in spite of the passing of time does not change. This something is what philosophers call the nature or essence of a thing, that which makes it what it is (a person, an animal, or a vegetable, for example). If you think about it, in any process of change unless there was some underlying element common to the before and after, that is, which links, for example, the baby Napoleon with the Emperor Napoleon, you would get a completely new being—which is obviously absurd. In short, as Aristotle rightly pointed out, in every change, there is something which changes and something which does not. Thus reality is composed of two elements: *nature* (or essence) and *adventure* (or change). Thus we can truthfully say that while human nature does not change—that which makes man a man (i.e. a rational animal as opposed to a dog or tree or stone) and which is common to all individual men everywhere and at all times—a particular human person does change, but *accidentally*, not essentially. For example, I can become more knowledgeable or fatter, but not more rational or more corporeal; for the amount of knowledge or weight I have are accidental properties, while rationality and corporeality belong to the nature or essence of man.

History (in its secondary sense) is one of the particular sciences, that is, it studies a *part* of reality. It is concerned with the development of human society through time. Furthermore, it studies historical change in terms of *secondary* or proximate causes, just as all the particular sciences do. Philosophy, by contrast, is concerned with the *whole* of reality, which it studies in terms of *ultimate*

Galileo (*left*) and Isaac Newton: astounding advances in knowledge

causes, that is, at the deepest level of reality. Thus it is concerned with both natures (or essences) and with adventure (or change). History and the other particular sciences (both the social sciences and the natural sciences) take their first principles for granted, such as, for instance, the existence of something called human nature (that all men, by essence, are rational animals), or the existence of cause and effect in the world. It is not their function to demonstrate these basic truths, even though they cannot do without them. It is the role of philosophy to demonstrate them.

Philosophy, however, is a difficult intellectual undertaking, demanding not only common sense and intelligence, but also humility (an openness to spiritual values) and a sound tradition. It can thus easily happen, as happened in Europe in the centuries following the Renaissance, that men become distracted from the higher truths by the more spectacular and more easily achieved discoveries of the natural sciences. It was the truly astounding advances in mathematics, physics and astronomy in the sixteenth and seventeenth centuries, due to the work of men like Copernicus, Galileo, and Isaac Newton, which made some thinkers conclude that now all knowledge lay within reach of human reason. The feeling of domination over nature had gone to their heads and blinded them to the fact that the exact sciences can only explain—and within definite limitations—what can be *measured* in the natural world, that is, what can be submitted to observation by the senses (with or without the help of instruments). They forgot that truths of the philosophical order, such as the truth that man is a composite of body and soul, whose physical and moral development depends on his following certain universal and unchanging natural laws, are altogether beyond the scope of the natural sciences, even though scientific observation can point towards the existence of such truths.

René Descartes (*top left*) treated philosophy like mathematics; Immanuel Kant (*top right*) treated philosophy like physics; Benedetto Croce treated philosophy like history, or history like philosophy

The unfortunate result of exaggerating the scope of the natural sciences was that philosophers developed an inferiority complex—as, incidentally, historians were to do in the twentieth century—and began trying to substitute for the methods of philosophy the methods of the particular sciences. Thus Descartes in the seventeenth century treated philosophy as if it was like mathematics, Kant in the eighteenth century treated it like physics, Comte and Marx and others in the nineteenth century as if it were like sociology or economics, and finally at the beginning of the twentieth century, Benedetto Croce and R. G. Collingwood, a pair of historian-philosophers, the one Italian, the other English—both much influenced by Hegel—treated philosophy as if it was history. Or, to put it more clearly still, they treated history as if it was the same as philosophy.

E. H. Carr is the unfortunate and perhaps unwitting heir of this unhealthy tradition of arbitrary substitutions, as can be seen in the following passage where he tries to justify the view that all values are historically conditioned, i.e. historicism in its second form.

> But the only point I wish to make at the moment is the impossibility of erecting an abstract and super-historical standard by which historical actions can be judged .... The attempt to erect such a standard is unhistorical and contradicts the very essence of history .... History is movement; and movement implies comparison. That is why historians tend to express their moral judgements in words of a comparative nature like 'progressive' and 'reactionary' rather than in uncompromising absolutes like 'good' and 'bad' ...

One might comment here that words like 'progressive' and 'reactionary' also convey moral approval and disapproval. Furthermore, even if the historian does speak mainly in comparative terms, it is impossible to say that one thing is more or less than another without having in mind a third absolute standard against which to judge the two being compared. For instance, if you say that modern Yoruba society is more just than nineteenth-century Yoruba society since in the latter domestic slavery was practised, you obviously have in mind an idea of justice which is absolute. If this were not so, there would be no way of justifying rationally our conviction that all forms of discrimination are wrong. Perhaps the best answer to Carr's apparent belief that the historian can be morally 'neutral' is the ironic one given by Professor Alfred Cobban when addressing a Conference of Historians in Ireland—a country with fresh memories of suffering under British colonialism:

> It is admittedly difficult ... to avoid 'the description of conduct in, generally speaking, moral terms'. This I take to mean that, for example, we cannot help describing the September massacres as massacres. The important thing is to avoid any suggestion that massacres are a bad thing, because this would be a moral judgement and therefore non-historical!

Carr's contention is that 'these supposedly absolute and extra-historical values ... are rooted in history' and that 'the practical content of hypothetical absolutes like equality, liberty, justice or natural law varies from period to period, or from continent to continent'. He fails to appreciate that a universal value such as justice, which can be defined as 'the virtue of giving each man his due', can be expressed in practice in many different ways, just as injustice can. Carr has fallen into the philosophical error of what Thomas Hobbes and others before him called 'nominalism', that is, the mistake of thinking that because you never see in concrete reality universal values such as 'justice', 'truth', humanity' etc., they are no more than artificially invented common 'names'.

The root of Carr's mistake is revealed in the statement: 'History has no funda-

Historical Explanation: The Heresy of Historicism

mental dependence on something outside itself which would differentiate it from any other science'. No particular science is independent of philosophy, that is, as regards its first principles, for the reasons explained earlier. If it tries to be, it runs the risk of distorting reality. The historian can indeed also be a philosopher, but if he wants to be one he must recognise that philosophy has its own

Alexander Solzhenitsyn: has Marxism been the ruin of his country?

aims and methods which are not only different from but also go beyond those of history and the particular sciences.

Finally it should be said that of all the historicist thinkers who have influenced history—in both senses—few have been more destructive than Karl Marx. The havoc wrought by the adoption of Marxist principles in countries such as Russia—the Russian statistician Professor Ivan Kurganov has estimated that between 1917 and 1957 Marxist socialism cost the Soviet Union 110 million lives—not to mention a large number of small nations such as Hungary, Czechoslovakia and, most recently, Vietnam, is evident to any one who looks closely at developments over the last few decades and does not let himself be deceived by propaganda. It is sufficient to read Alexander Solzhenitsyn's *Gulag Archipelago*: an account—based partly on personal experience and partly on documents—of the 'sewage disposal' system which has been operating in Russia since the early days of Stalin for the crushing of all those suspected of raising the slightest objection to the communist dictatorship. Solzhenitsyn, who himself spent some eleven years as a political prisoner in the forced labour camps of Siberia, knew what he was talking about when he said in early 1976 that Marxism had been the ruin of his country.

Marxism is much more than a theory that in history economic factors are the most important, and that 'progress' is the result of the clash of opposing social classes struggling to control the means of production. It is an attempt at a total explanation of the whole of reality, and one which seeks not only to interpret the world—as other philosophies have traditionally done—but also to change it. Marxism is thus both a philosophy and a religion, although a religion with God thrown out.

The centrepieces of Marx's thought are his dialectical materialism and his historical materialism, two closely linked notions not easy to explain. For Marx and his friend and collaborator, Engels, did not reach their conclusions about reality either from a study of history or from a study of economics, but from a study of recent philosophy, particularly Hegelian philosophy. As Engels said: 'We have arrived at communism only by way of the dissolution of Hegelian speculation carried out by Feuerbach. But the true living conditions of the proletariat are unknown to us'. (Feuerbach, by the way, was the atheistic philospher who did most to convince Marx and Engels of the advantages of making man, not God, the centre of the universe.)

The major influence upon Marx and Engels, however, was Hegel. From him they derived the theory of the dialectic and the typical historicist prejudice that reality is fundamentally change, movement, that is, history. 'We know only one science: the science of history,' wrote Engels in 1845 in the *German Ideology*. But unlike Hegel—whom Engels claimed to have stood upon his head—Marx and Engels assumed that the sole foundation of all reality was matter, not spirit or idea or reason, as Hegel had asserted. Thus Marx and Engels assumed—without troubling to prove it—that all change in history was due solely to material, that is, economic factors. According to them the base or 'infrastructure' of human society is entirely material or economic. Such elements as law, political institutions, the arts and sciences, philosophy and religion, etc., are no more than a 'superstructure', of quite secondary importance because they entirely depend on and derive from the economic base.

Now the logical consequence of believing that everything, including man, is material, is that you must also believe that everything, including man, is entirely subject to the laws of nature; in other words, everything that happens in the world, in history, is 'determined' and 'necessary'. This is Marx's justification for considering the study of history a science, as being a study of laws. For Marx and Engels historical materialism was in fact primarily a method which consisted in looking for

> the final cause and decisive propelling force behind all important historical events in the economic development of society, in the transformations of the system of production and exchange, in the consequent division of society into distinct classes and in the struggles of these classes amongst themselves. (Engels, *From Utopian Socialism to Scientific Socialism*.)

In short, the materialism Marx and Engels inherited from Feuerbach and others compelled them logically to deny human freedom as one of the causes of historical change, since only a creature with spiritual powers—of intellect and will—can be said to be free.

The question next arises for the Marxist: what then is the secret of history, that is, the fundamental law which explains all change and which if discovered can not only explain the past but also the future? The answer is: Hegel's theory of the dialectic. The dialectic is a process of change, or rather *the* process of change (to which the whole of reality is subject) on the basis of the clash of opposites. In Hegel's philosophy it meant that one idea—for him the dialectic was primarily a process of thought, of logic—inevitably engendered its opposite (for example, freedom implies its opposite, namely discipline or control). The two ideas then clash and from the clash emerges a synthesis of the two, representing a step forward to a higher stage which incorporates the best elements of the earlier stage. The new idea then engenders a further opposing idea, and the whole process of a thesis, antithesis, synthesis is repeated, many times in fact, until eventually a final perfect synthesis is achieved, the stage in which the Absolute Idea becomes fully conscious of itself, having absorbed in the course of its historical development everything into itself.

This extremely abstract process, Hegel thought, was represented in concrete human history under the form of the Idea of Freedom. Human progress was nothing other than 'the development of the consciousness of freedom on the part of Spirit, and of the consequent realisation of that freedom'. This law of progress Hegel saw exemplified in actual history by the transition from the ancient oriental civilisations (China, Babylonia and Egypt) in which only the monarch—all his subjects being slaves of some sort—was free through Graeco-Roman civilisation in which the whole citizen body—although not the slaves—enjoyed freedom, to contemporary Germanic Protestant Europe in which due to Christianity the infinite worth of every individual man was recognised. On the political level the modern nation state in fact represented for Hegel the peak of human development, as being one of the most crucial 'stages' of the development of the Idea or Spirit as a whole.

Marx took over the theory of the dialectic—with only a few minor modifications— but in place of the 'nation state' as the key social unit in human history he put the social 'class'. He thus saw history as the history of class warfare. For instance, in medieval Europe the landed feudal aristocracy engendered its opposite, namely the exploited landless peasantry. The clash between the two classes led to the overthrow of the feudal aristocracy and their substitution by the town-based merchant and industrial class (i.e. the capitalist bourgeois class) who later engendered their opposite, namely the exploited industrial worker class or proletariat. Next, Marx predicted, the proletariat would rise up and overthrow the exploiting bourgeois capitalist class, abolish all private property—according to him the chief source of strife—and, after a period of proletarian dictatorship, the state would wither away altogether leaving behind a blissful classless society in which all men were happy.

Both Hegel and Marx found themselves involved in at least one major theoretical contradiction—that is, leaving aside the travesty of historical facts their interpretation of the past often led to. If the law of the dialectic was immutable and inevitable, what need for men to do anything except wait for history to take its course? Hegel and Marx deny human freedom, but nonetheless expect men to collaborate with the dialectic. To this Marxists reply that it is not theory which justifies practice, but practice which justifies the theory; so that if the practice does not fit the theory, you must modify the theory. This of course involves further contradictions. But a full discussion of these problems cannot be entered into here.

Examples of Marxist professional history are Endre Sik's *The History of Black Africa* (produced in two volumes in an English translation by the Akademiai Kiado, Budapest, 1966) and the U.S.S.R. Academy of Sciences (Institute of Africa) production by a team of scholars entitled *A History of Africa 1918–1967* (Moscow, 1968). Both works interpret African history in terms of the 'class struggle' and as following the typical Marxist steps or stages through which every society is supposed to pass on its way towards the overthrow of the 'bourgeoisie' by the 'proletariat' before the abolition of private property and the eventual withering away of the state altogether.

Endre Sik divides his first volume into four parts corresponding to some of the first 'stages': 1. Black Africa prior to the European Intrusion. 2. Black Africa in the Age of Primitive Accumulation. 3. Black Africa in the period of Industrial Capitalism. 4. Black Africa in the period of the Transition of Capitalism into Imperialism. In his Introduction (p. 19) he claims that 'A study of the history of Black Africa brilliantly substantiates and most vividly illustrates a whole series of theses maintained by Marx, Lenin and Stalin in the field of historical science'. He also claims (pp. 15 and 16) that 'the intellectual and moral qualities of any particular human being, as well as the national characteristics of peoples, are ... products of their social and economic development', and that 'the historic

Historical Explanation: The Heresy of Historicism

destinies of peoples are determined ... by the degree of development of the productive forces' (i.e. economic materialism).

The other work mentioned above has an almost identical approach, though focusing on a more limited period of time. It abounds in phrases such as 'the struggle of the African masses against imperialist exploitation' (p. 322) and 'the conflict between the national bourgeoisie and the foreign monopolies' (p. 18), and gives prominence to the role of communist-inspired groups or parties such as The Socialist Workers' and Farmers' Party of Nigeria. In the Introduction (p. 26) it claims that 'The working class is marching in the front ranks of the fighters for national and social progress .... In the African countries which have won independence, the working class is undergoing an accelerating ideological and political schooling and is swiftly throwing off the influence of bourgeois and patriarchal-peasant ideology.' One of Endre Sik's main conclusions is similarly that imperialism changed the millions of African peoples into revolutionary peasants, and '... brought into being its own grave-digger—the revolutionary proletariat' (p. 319, vol. 2).

In neither work, however, is much effort made to substantiate these sweeping generalisations with historical evidence. In the great majority of African countries, even now, the industrial working class is still a very small percentage of the total population, and one certainly gets the impression that the so-called 'masses' or peasants continue for the most part very little interested in 'revolution', if not indeed actually opposed to it, as are the 'masses' in most parts of the world including Soviet Russia.

Let it only be said in conclusion that appealing as Marxist denunciations of capitalism and all forms of exploitation often sound—indeed these exploitations certainly require denunciation—the Marxist solutions proposed lead to even greater exploitation, since they assume as the principle of progress inevitable conflict. At bottom Marxism 'is based on an intellectual swindle', to quote Eric Voegelin's penetrating *Science, Politics and Gnosticism*, since it is a deliberate attempt to distort reality. This is why Marxist historicism is not only a heresy, but of the most dangerous type: it reduces man to the status of a slave. It also seduces historians into forcing upon historical events an interpretation which, while it certainly contains some elements of truth, gives an overall picture which is false. This is inevitable since the criterion of 'good' Marxist historical writing is not objective truth—however difficult that may be to achieve in practice—but conformity to the official Marxist line.

For further reading

BARRACLOUGH, GEOFFREY, *History in a Changing World*, University of Oklahoma, 1956.
BOCHENSKI, J. M., *Soviet Russian Dialectical Materialism (Diamat)*, D. Reidel Publishing Company, Dordrecht, Holland, 1963, chs. 1 and 2.
DAWSON, CHRISTOPHER, *The Dynamics of World History*, (ed. John Mulloy), Sheed and Ward, London, 1957, the chapter on Marx.

DAWSON, CHRISTOPHER, *Progress and Religion*, Sheed and Ward, London, 1934, chs. 1 and 2.
WALSH, W. H. *Introduction to Philosophy of History*, Hutchinson University Library, London, 1967, chs. 7 and 8.
WRIGLEY, CHRISTOPHER, 'Historicism in Africa', *African Affairs*, xx, 279, April 1971.